The heart of the prairie

John Mackie

THE NEW HAVERSACKS

THE HEART OF THE PRAIRIE

A Merry Christmas
To Donal

from Stewart

I PICKED MYSELF UP QUICKER THAN EVER I PICKED
MYSELF UP IN MY LIFE

THE HEART
OF THE PRAIRIE

BY

JOHN MACKIE

AUTHOR OF " A BUSH MYSTERY " "HIDDEN IN
CANADIAN WILDS" ETC. ETC.

London

NISBET & CO. LTD.
22 BERNERS STREET, W.1

PRINTED IN GREAT BRITAIN BY
MORRISON AND GIBB LTD., LONDON AND EDINBURGH
P 2033

PREFACE

NOT so many years ago, when the facilities for travel were different from what they are now, a great deal of rubbish and erroneous impressions were disseminated by so called literature purporting to deal with adventures and phases of life in certain little-known places of the earth. There are some authors who still think that no matter how absurd and misleading their local colouring may be, the pictorial element is everything. I venture to think otherwise. In my rolling-stone experience I have found fact much stranger than fiction, and have gleaned from real life and nature a knowledge of men and things which stands me in better stead than any flight of the imagination—useful to weavers of stories as that faculty is.

I can, at least, claim truthfulness of detail for this story, as I lived for some years in that wild and fascinating portion of "The Great Lone Land," described in these pages, as a mounted police officer in charge of that part of the frontier So, the cowboys, the mounted policemen, the Indians, and even the bears and the smugglers, are all old friends of mine.

JOHN MACKIE.

TABLE OF CONTENTS

CHAPTER VII.

PAGE

CHAPTER VIII.

CHAPTER IX.

CHAPTER X.

CHAPTER XI.

CHAPTER XII.

CHAPTER XIII.

CHAPTER XIV.

CONTENTS.

CHAPTER XV

CHAPTER XVI.

CHAPTER XVII.

CHAPTER XVIII.

CHAPTER XIX.

CHAPTER XX.

CHAPTER XXI.

CHAPTER XXII.

CHAPTER XXIII.

CHAPTER XXIV.

CHAPTER XXV

THE
HEART OF THE PRAIRIE.

CHAPTER I.

A RUDE AWAKENING.

I, WALTER DERRINGHAM, was sixteen years of age, and had come home from Harrow for my summer holidays. Perhaps I should not use the word "home," for my real one had been broken up years before on the death of my father and mother, so when not at school I lived with an uncle, Gilbert Derringham, a well-to-do, middle-aged bachelor, at his comfortable old country house in Middlesex. He loved to slip through life so quietly, and was so accustomed to getting his own way, that no one dreamt he would risk his independence by taking to himself a life-partner. When one day, however, he married a society-loving widow, who was reported to have a mind and very decided opinions of her own, and who had, moreover, a family of three, it must be confessed that I, like many more, was considerably astonished, and felt not a little sore on the subject. Indeed, my

B

uncle's old housekeeper, Nanny, who had been
with him for twenty years, felt so aggrieved that
she gave notice to leave on the spot. I fancy
my uncle was rather surprised, when the day
came, that she actually did leave, for he had not
been accustomed to take his old housekeeper
seriously, and it is unlikely it ever crossed his
simple mind that the best of servants do not
care about changes, more particularly when
they have been accustomed to consider themselves their own mistresses.

As for the two other servants, they waited
until my uncle brought home his wife, and then
they too gave notice. It was quite evident to
them that their days of peace and plenty were
over; as they were real good sorts one could
not help feeling sorry for them. But, at the
same time, I did not exactly care about the
mysterious and aggravating manner which they
thought fit to adopt towards me. They were
kind in a way that was positively painful; all
the good spirits seemed to have left them, and
with sad headshakings they would refer vaguely
to certain scheming usurpers, and the altered
nature of what they chose to consider my
" prospects." I remember they were far from
being complimentary to their master, and on
more than one occasion I overheard them speak
of him as " that old fool." At the time, I considered their attitude was most unjust and
unkind; now it is evident to me they knew my
poor uncle better than I did. This admission

may savour of ingratitude, but having at least on one occasion overheard Gilbert Derringham admit as much himself, it is not altogether inexcusable.

The woman he married was unprincipled and scheming, and from the moment she came to the Cedars showed herself in her true colours, particularly to those whose good graces she did not think it worth while to cultivate. Still, she seemed to exercise some mysterious influence over my uncle; for never have I seen a good man so much the slave and the cat's-paw of a bad woman. It often puzzled me to think how a man, whom I knew to be generous and honourable, could give in to a woman's projects which in his heart he must have condemned.

I was not at the marriage, but when I stood at the hall door with a few others to welcome my uncle and his wife on their home-coming, I felt instinctively that the Cedars was no longer my home, and that I was considered an intruder. Mrs. Gilbert Derringham might have been good-looking once upon a time, but when she looked one up and down sharply, with those hard, calculating blue eyes of hers, I wondered what a man could see in a mere mask of flesh and blood, with nothing behind it but what was soulless and sordid. She was socially ambitious, and my elders have told me that some women will sacrifice everything to this fetish, especially those who are not by nature ladies.

She must have begun soon to carry things with a high hand, for within a few days she made my position plain to me in the presence of my uncle. Her assumed air of kindliness and candour never for a moment deceived me if it did Gilbert Derringham, who, it must be admitted, seemed rather ashamed of the interview which I will now relate.

She was loth to speak to me so soon, she said, but thought it only kindness to let me know my exact position. She did not know whether or not I was aware that all that was left to me of my deceased father's estate was a number of worthless shares in a Queensland gold mine, which for years had yielded no dividends, and which, indeed, was being worked at a loss in the pursuit of a forlorn hope. Perhaps I was not aware that I had all along been living upon the charity of my uncle.

Gilbert Derringham here lifted his hands deprecatingly, and as if to stop her, but the woman went on.

That had been all very well so long as my uncle was unmarried, but now that he had new responsibilities, it was not to be expected that he could afford to pay the heavy expenses of a public school any longer. I was now in my seventeenth year; did I not think it was time to go out into the world and do something for myself, seeing that I could hardly expect the same help as heretofore?

I turned hot and cold on hearing these things.

I had always been morbidly sensitive, and my pride had received a severe shock. My uncle looked ashamed and decidedly ill at ease. I think he was going to say something, but his wife looked at him, and the words died upon his lips. What followed is not particularly edifying. I lost my temper, and told his wife if I had lived upon my uncle's charity it had been done in ignorance of my true position. He had allowed me to think that the money he gave me, and what he paid for my education, was only what was due to me from my poor father's estate. It had been done out of his goodness of heart, but it had turned out cruelly for me. I would take nothing from either of them any longer, and so far as she, my uncle's wife, was concerned, her motives were obvious enough; she wanted to send her two sons to school, and was afraid there would not be money enough for all of us. I wound up by saying that as she had lost no time in showing her hand, and had taken such an evident pleasure in putting the truth before me as brutally as possible, I made no apology for speaking as I did.

I never before in my life had spoken so plainly to anyone, and it sometimes puzzles me to know where my courage came from. I seemed to have changed from a boy into a man on being brought face to face with the grim reality of her words. For the moment Mrs. Derringham seemed so taken aback by my boldness that she was incapable of speech. My

2

uncle looked more distressed than ever, but I
had sense enough to know that he was in the
woman's power and so hurried from the room.
Had my two half-cousins been like some of my
late school companions I would have gone to
them at once and told them of my troubles; but
although there was not a great deal of difference
in our ages, they aped the ways of men in a
manner that was ludicrous, and seemed to prefer
the companionship of stable-boys and grooms to
that of their social equals, so they were not to
be thought of.

I was passing through a side door to my
favourite nook in the plantation when I almost
ran against my third new cousin, whose existence, I admit, till then had hardly given me a
thought. Properly speaking, she was not Mrs.
Derringham's daughter, but a dead brother's
child who had left her fairly well off, and it was
currently supposed that it was her income
which had kept the whole family going until her
scheming aunt's second marriage. She was
about the same age as myself, and had what I
considered to be red hair. There was certainly
lots of it, and though I had heard my uncle say
it was very wonderful hair and much admired
by people who knew about such matters, it
would be outside the truth to say that I did.
She was a shy girl, with large hazel eyes which
gave one the idea that she was always terribly
in earnest and thinking of all sorts of things.
I fancy there was something in it, when people

said they were fine eyes. There could be no doubt about the clearness and the softness of her skin; but that could only have appealed to girls who put such an incomprehensible value on complexions: such a thing could hardly interest me, a boy. She had hitherto barely spoken to me, but I liked the look in her eyes; they seemed to say such a lot, and I felt certain that, despite the colour of her hair, she was a nice girl.

I expected she would stand aside shyly to let me pass, and so she did at first; but the moment she looked into my face with those great, uncanny eyes of hers, I never saw such a change come over a girl in my life. Her painful embarrassment left her in a moment, and she stepped right in front of me.

"Let me pass," I demanded, somewhat sulkily, I daresay.

"Walter," she said softly and perfectly at her ease, "won't you tell me about it? Has Mrs. Derringham been saying anything to you? I know she has—Oh, what a shame! I didn't think she would have the courage to."

"She got something back that she didn't quite like, anyhow!" I interrupted, watching the girl's face curiously. It had not struck me before that there was so much in it, and she really had wonderful eyes. That was doubtless why she was able to sum up the situation at a glance. Whichever way it was, there was something so genuine and kindly in her manner that I could not pass by without appearing to notice her as I had at first intended.

"What did you say to her?" asked the girl anxiously.

"Oh! it's a long story and wouldn't interest you!" I replied. "By the way, what's your name? I forget it."

I somehow began to think I should like to know her name; there was something so frank and honest about her. I began to feel sorry that she was only a girl, and not a boy. Otherwise, I am sure she would have made a splendid chum.

Why a smile should have dawned and rippled over the girl's face when I asked this simple question I cannot say. But there is no accounting for a girl's fancy. However, she pulled herself up short and tried to look serious. I noticed, for the first time, that there was a mole like a beauty spot on her left cheek, and two wonderful dimples in the neighbourhood of her chin; I never thought before that dimples could be nice to look at. To remind her of the fact that I had asked a simple question, I again inquired her name.

"Muriel," she replied, "but surely it cannot interest you!"

She had used my own words and paid me back in my own coin just as a boy would have done. I thought it rather plucky of her, so told her in as few words as possible what had occurred. She seemed greatly interested and

never once interrupted me. When I had
finished, she rather abruptly asked,—

"What are you going to do, Walter?"

"Clear out," I replied, "and at once. If
they won't let me, I'll run away."

"Come into the garden, she said, "and talk
it over. I know where there's such a jolly quiet
place."

CHAPTER II.

CAS1 ON MY OWN RESOURCES.

THE girl's name was Muriel Wray, and I some. how felt glad that it was not Derringham. When she slipped her arm into mine in order to lead me to the quiet place she spoke about in the garden, I thought it was rather like taking liberties, seeing she was only a girl. But she seemed so very friendly towards me, and there was something else about her—something that I cannot quite describe, but which put me in mind of looking at a very beautiful flower, and was soothing and restful to my stormy frame of mind just then—that made me go passively with her. At the same time, if I had met my half-cousins or even a man-servant, I would un-doubtedly have freed her arm from mine. I thought it was so silly of a boy to be seen going about in such a chummy fashion with a girl, even although that girl was what might be called pretty.

We reached the lonely spot she spoke about, which was simply an old summer-house at the far end of the garden, overlooking a little stream, and she led me into it, sitting down opposite. The little table was between us, but I hoped that no one would come and find us there; I always hated being chaffed about girls.

Muriel Wray broke the silence by saying that I was talking nonsense about going away all at once; neither my uncle nor my new aunt dreamt that I should do such a thing. Of course I could stop at the Cedars until I had made up my mind as to my future career, and then go off to London, or elsewhere, like any other sensible young fellow. I might have to board with people or go into lodgings while I was learning my business, but that was a matter of course. She knew Mrs. Derringham was exaggerating my poverty when she declared that I was utterly dependent on my uncle. She had heard that I had interests which might at any time bring me in lots of money.

I did not know until long afterwards that Muriel had gone to my uncle and tried to persuade him to use some of her own means on my behalf, on the sole condition that he was never to say a word about it to anyone.

As for my running away, she expressed the hope that I would do nothing so foolish. When I told her that the one great ambition of my life was to travel in strange countries, and ex-perience some of the wonderful adventures I had read about, the warm blood mounted into her white skin for a moment, and her eyes gleamed like two stars. I went on to say that if I were condemned to sit on a three-legged stool in a musty office, I would never have any such opportunities, and that even if I became rich as a Rothschild, I should still regret not having followed my natural bent.

The girl's small hands twitched nervously on her lap, and her eyes wandered away to the opposite bank, as I spoke like this. I believe that in her heart the girl was brimming over with romance, and that had she been a boy she would not have hesitated one moment to pursue the course I now meditated. But it is my belief that with that odd vein of practicality, which I am told some women possess, she advised me against what she herself would have chosen for my own good. As I watched her sitting, looking out into the dim depths of the pine wood opposite with a thoughful look in her eyes, I began to wonder how it was I had hitherto seemed to look upon her only as a girl who was hardly worth the passing notice of a boy in his seventeenth year. She seemed to have suddenly grown ever so much older than myself, and when a little shaft of sunlight straggled in through the lattice-work, and flooded the silky tangles of her hair as with a glory, I wondered how I could ever have called it red and seen no beauties in it. Red it was not; it reminded one of that rare, soft, golden tinge that the setting sun leaves behind it in the fleecy clouds after the rain. I began to be rather ashamed of having treated her in such an off-hand way, and I wondered if she had noticed it. The situation, I fancied, required some explanation.

I cleared my throat to attract her attention and said something, but what it was it is impossible for me now to remember. I came to a dead stop, conscious of having wandered from the point, and thought she looked at me with a gleam of awakened interest in her eyes.

"I'm afraid I haven't explained myself very clearly," I observed, wondering what it was I had said, and feeling my utter inability to explain the delicate nature of what was in my mind.

"Then, I wouldn't trouble to, if I were you," she rejoined, laughingly. "I really didn't think there was anything rude in your manner towards me. I did think you were just a trifle awkward, but when you know me better you won't be: boys generally like me."

"I should fancy they did," I said, in a sudden burst of frankness, and then I pulled myself up short, and found myself thinking that it was an awful piece of cheek on the part of the other boys to like her. It was doubtless natural enough on their part, but it seemed to me that if I should get to like her very much, I would not care about sharing her with other fellows.

In a few minutes more I was talking to her just as if she had been an old school-fellow; it was difficult to believe that a girl should know so much, and seem to enter so heartily into the plans and projects of a boy. In a quarter of an

hour I had agreed to respect the powers that
were, and not do anything rash, until at least I
had proof positive they were going to force me
into some line of life utterly unsuited to my
tastes.

We must have been some considerable time
in that summer-house, although strangely enough
I hardly noticed it ; for she told me a good deal
about herself that considerably interested me,
and it seemed to give me an odd sort of consola-
tion to think there were others who felt a good
deal alone in the world, and who accordingly
had to make the best of things.   I began to think
that girls were not so very bad after all, and
that she had not bored me in the least.   It was
she who first rose to go, and then I felt myself
in an awkward fix, as all my old prejudices
sprang into life again.   I didn't care to be seen
going with the girl to the house.   When she
looked up into my face with those wonderful
eyes of hers, I could have sworn she guessed my
thoughts, for she came towards me, and holding
out her hand as if to ratify our agreement, said—

" Now, don't forget your promise. You needn't
trouble to come to the house with me.   I'll see
you again at dinner.   Be good to yourself till
then."   It was as good as a glimpse of sunshine
to see the cheerfulness on her face.

I took her hand, sheepishly enough no doubt,
as she came close up to me and looked into my
face with an odd, half shy look of inquiry in it.
There was something in that look that sent the

blood tingling through my veins, and for the life
of me I could not tell why. I had never until
that moment imagined that any face could be so
beautiful, and there was such a world of sympathy
in her eyes, that for the moment I felt myself
the slave of an unreasoning impulse. I caught
up her hand in my two, drawing her slightly
towards me, and then as her eyes dropped
before mine, I took sudden fright and released
her. Now that I think of it, she must have
thought me an awful fool, I know now that I had
never before come so near kissing a girl.

When she had gone I sat down again, and it
was as if a new interest had come into my life.
I had always felt very much alone in the world,
for my uncle, although kind to me, seemed ever-
lastingly engrossed in his own pursuits; and
what with having no one older than myself to
talk to and advise me as to my future, it is more
than likely less thought was bestowed on the
matter than is usual with boys of my age. I
had been an insatiable reader of books of travel
and adventure, and I had never entertained any
idea other than that of leading an out-of-door,
free, stirring existence. Moreover, having got
it into my head that there was no occasion to
trouble about the future in a worldly sense, I had
not that insight into my capabilities and dis-
qualifications that other boys usually have, who
are impressed with the fact that they must depend
entirely upon their own exertions to gain a
livelihood. Perhaps my uncle was not a little

to blame in the matter, but doubtless he had meant well. I know now that it is the greatest curse that can befall a boy to bring him up in the knowledge that his future is assured. Whether it is or not, the greatest blessing and legacy that a parent or guardian can confer upon a child is a clear understanding and appreciation of that sovereign remedy, Work. I had lived in a world of books and dreams, and had lost sight of the stern practicalities of life. It was but natural that I should have my views corrected in the world of which I knew so little. The base metal must be separated from the true ore sooner or later, and that means the refiner's fire.

But to be brief, Mrs. Derringham had prevailed upon my uncle to find a situation for me in a lawyer's office in the city. This was done without consulting my inclinations in the slightest, and though my uncle, when he told me the news, was somewhat shamefaced, and hinted vaguely about finding something better for me later on, I felt that the time had come to shift for myself. I felt that an indoor life, such as was proposed, was something quite irreconcilable with my nature. I thanked my uncle for all his past kindness to me and begged him either to find some out-of-door work, to let me go out and take my chance in the Colonies, or let me shift for myself. I believe he would have given in to my wishes if it had not been for his wife, for she at once tried to ridicule what she called the unreasonableness and absurdity of my plans, accused me of ingratitude, and began to exercise a series of mean, little restraints over me that was galling in the extreme. Even her sons would have nothing to do with me, and I believe they were only prevented from showing their dislike in a more marked fashion by the obvious fact that I was rather a strong, well-set-up lad for my years, and would be likely to resent an insult.

For the next few weeks my life would have been unbearable had it not been for Muriel Wray. We had become great friends, and I could not believe that a girl could have entered into a boy's life and ways as she did. Had any one told me a few weeks before that I would become so chummy with a girl, I would have hit them. I admit that I would have run away long before I did, if it had not been for her. She advised me to be patient, and I knew that she had even spoke to my uncle himself about me. On one occasion she proved herself no coward, for Mrs. Derringham saying something to me a little more bitter than usual, caused her to speak out on my behalf; and she did it in such a plucky way that my views regarding girls were altered considerably. What also surprised me was the spirit in which Mrs. Derringham seemed to take her self-possessed words of disapproval. While she did not actually appear to fear Muriel Wray, she yet seemed disinclined to arouse her anger. I afterwards learned that she had very good reasons for assuming this attitude. Muriel

Wray was at least mistress of her own income, and Mrs. Derringham owed her a considerable sum of money. The scheming woman also contemplated a marriage later on with her eldest son, so as to have a greater hold upon her.

But things came to a crisis at last. One day I told Muriel that I would like to see her after lunch in the old summer-house, as I had something important to communicate. I daresay it was weak and silly of me, but I still did not care that people should see us, a boy and girl, so friendly. I daresay she was secretly amused over my weakness, but fell in with my ways unquestioningly. She never cared what people thought or said about her; she was one of the pluckiest creatures, boy or girl, I ever met in my life. She was now in my sight quite as worthy of consideration as any boy.

What I meant to tell Muriel Wray was that on the following night I meant to leave my uncle's home, make my way to London, get on a ship going abroad, and strike out for myself. I had no very decided plans, but I at least had made up my mind that go I would, without any further delay.

CHAPTER III.

"I RUN AWAY."

I HAD not been long in the old summer-house before Muriel Wray came. It was a warm July day, and she was dressed all in soft fleecy white. I know now that dark colours were her favourite ones, and suited her best, but I did not know anything about such things in those days, and of late I had begun to think that she always looked well in anything. Even to my untutored senses there was an air of finish and daintiness about her that possessed some indefinable charm. She, doubtless, saw at a glance that something very serious was the matter with me, but she did not affect a concern she could hardly be expected to feel. In a quiet matter-of-fact way she said,

"What is it, Walter? Tell me all about it."

I did, and it amounted to this. My uncle had told me, in the presence of my aunt, that within a week I was to be prepared to take up my residence in London, as he had found an opening for me in a solicitor's office, and I would be duly articled within the next few days. Again there was an unavailing appeal on my part, and when

it was received with contempt, I somewhat in-
discreetly remarked that I would take good care
never to cross that solicitor's threshold. Whereupon I was forbidden to leave the grounds until
such time as it came for me to take my departure.
To cut a long story short, I had secretly gone to
my room, over-hauled my small stock of personal effects, wrote a letter to my uncle which
would be found next day on my dressing-table;
put such clothes as I would be likely to need
into a small black bag, and finally resolved that
as soon as the family had retired for the night, I
would quietly depart to seek my fortune in
foreign lands. I knew it was not a nice thing to
do, to steal out of my uncle's house at dead of
night, like a thief, but no other course was open
to me. They would not let me go of my own
free will, and I hated making a fuss.

Muriel Wray waited patiently until I had
finished, and then by every argument she could
think of, she tried to shake my determination.
It must be confessed some of the questions she
put rather staggered me. Where did I intend
going? What training and knowledge had I to
prepare me for the plunge into a rough, wide-
awake world? And lastly, what money had I to
enable me to get out of the country?

The money question was what cornered me,
for I had only a five-pound note in the world.

"Then you've got to take a loan from me,"
she said, when she saw that I was determined to
go. "Only a twenty-pound note, and you must

promise to write and tell me how you are getting on, and I will write to you."

But it was only when I plainly enough saw that the good-hearted girl would be deeply hurt by my refusal, that I consented to take the money, on the distinct understanding that it was to be repaid.

I confess that during this interview I had to keep my head turned away from Muriel Wray, lest the sight of her wistful eyes might turn me from my purpose. My friends always considered me of a disposition not likely to be easily moved. In reality I was impressionable to a degree, only it went against the grain to be demonstrative.

Muriel Wray insisted on being up to say good-bye to me that night when I left. I was not going to leave the old place, she said, as if I were an outcast, without a friend in the world. There need be no difficulties in the way. It was a large, old-fashioned house, and our rooms were both in the same wing; a separate staircase, and a door at the far end of the passage were pretty certain to be free from interruption. When it struck twelve on the old clock over the entrance to the stables, and it was safe to hazard that the household was asleep, it would be time for me to be off.

We discussed many things in regard to the future, in a somewhat sad and half-hearted way, and then the girl took her departure.

I shall never forget as long as I live the pain it occasioned me to go round the old place, and

3

say good-bye to everything : for I had looked
upon the Cedars as my home, and the familiar
surroundings of our boyhood make a deeper im-
pression than those which come with the years.
I confess I almost cried on looking for the last
time at the pigeons on the stable roof, on patting
each of the horses, and allowing Cæsar, the old
watch-dog, to push his cold nose into my hands.
I was glad when it was all over; I had hardly
thought that parting from my dumb friends
could be so bitter.

How that evening passed it is not difficult to
remember now.   All preparations for my departure had been made, and my condition was one
of feverish excitement as the hours wore on.   I
really felt sorry to leave my uncle Gilbert in the
way I intended ; for despite the stern measures
he had of late adopted towards me, I knew they
were not the outcome of his own inclinations.
There was still a very soft spot in my heart for
him, and that evening in the drawing-room I
tried to show this by being as attentive to him
as possible.   As for Muriel Wray, she sat in a
great chair apparently reading, but I knew well
she did very little of that, for the expression on
her face was subdued and thoughtful, and several
times I caught her looking at me over the top of
her book.   Once or twice she made an evident
effort to rally and say something cheerful, but
the result was anything but successful.   When
I thought of this afterwards I felt rather glad
that it was so.   I was very thankful indeed when

that last evening at the Cedars came to an end.

With what an ominous deliberation the old clock at the stables struck the twelve hours that night! To me each stroke seemed full of prophecy, and to herald the beginning of a new life. And a new life truly it was to be, for when the hammer fell for the last time I realised that the past was done with for ever, and the new life with all its possibilities had begun.

I rose from the bed on which I had flung myself; made sure that one precious relic, a small locket which had belonged to my mother, hung safely on my breast inside my shirt, and then—and the boy who is ashamed to say as much is a fool—I knelt down by my bedside and said my prayers. Picking up my slender belongings in the small black bag, I went on tip-toe along the corridor and down the old-fashioned, winding stairs.

Muriel Wray had said she would be up to see me off, but surely it was more than one could expect. She was only a girl after all, and girls were always saying things they did not mean. Perhaps she repented of that burst of generosity in which she begged me to accept the loan of a twenty-pound note : girls often did such unaccountable things.

I was heartily ashamed of such thoughts before they had almost passed through my mind, for in the moonlight that streamed into the hall from the fan-light above the door, I saw the shadowy figure of the girl. I approached her without speaking ; in another moment she had caught me by the hand, and, bringing her face close to mine, whispered :—

" Think better of it, Walter—think better of it. No one need be the wiser if you change your mind now. You don't know what you're going to do."

There was something like a catch in her breath as she spoke these words, and it required all my courage to resist them.

"Come outside into the Lime Walk," I replied, " we can speak better there."

We passed into the bright moonlight and the warm summer's night, and soon were out of sight of the house.

"Now we have gone far enough," I said, "but, Muriel, I can't go back. I've gone so far now that the thing's impossible. I'm not a girl——"

Then I stopped short and doubtless looked foolish as I saw her great, dark eyes gazing wonderingly into mine. But she ignored the latter part of my speech, and it was the best way in which she could have punished me.

" If you find you don't get on, and things go wrong with you, Walter, will you come back ? Don't let your pride stand in the way of your future. Remember your uncle is really very fond of you, and would be only too glad to have you back. As for Mrs. Derringham, you need not consider her in the matter at all."

I told her that such a course was impossible.

Unless I could come back with an assured competency or position I could never come at all; but I hoped to come back. And looking at her the desire to make my fortune and prove myself no weakling was very strong within me. As I spoke, it seemed to me that for a moment a pleased look struggled through the wistfulness on her face; but it was gone again, just as a ray of sunlight is lost in a weary sky. It was quite evident to me, although she did not say so, that she was not over sanguine in regard to my future. But it was time to be off.

"I must be going," I observed. "Let me see you back to the house."

But she would not hear of it.

"I can go back quite well by myself," she said. "There is just one thing more I want to speak to you about, and I am sure you won't mind me speaking about it, Walter, you see, there's no one else to do it. Promise me you'll always walk straight, and never do a mean or dishonourable action?"

I felt hurt for the moment, but the girl had caught my hands in hers, and was gazing steadily into my eyes. Her face was very close to mine. It was impossible to be angry with her; she was obviously sincere, and so terribly in earnest.

"Yes," I replied, "I promise you." And the memory of that promise kept me straight more than once in my stormy after-life, when I was sorely tempted to take advantage of the moment, without considering whether I was pursuing a strictly honourable course or not.

As we shook hands she pushed a small packet into my jacket pocket. "It's the loan, Walter," she observed, "if you never repay it, it won't matter in the least, and should you want more, you've only to write to me. I've got more than I require."

I wrung her hand and turned to go, but she still held my hands. I looked into her great, brown eyes and saw something suspiciously like tears in them. I wondered why she delayed me, but the next moment I learned the reason.

"Won't you kiss me, Walter?" she asked. And I did; and now that I think of it, this thought is borne home to me. Had it not been for Muriel Wray and her disinterested love for me, I might have gone into the world that night a veritable Ishmael, and with the spirit of Ishmael in my heart : with the thought that there was not a human being who cared for me or who had the slightest interest in my life. I almost fear to think of what might have happened had this been so.

When I had kissed her, I turned away with a great lump in my throat, unable to say a single word, and made off through the trees. I turned when I had gone some fifteen or twenty yards and looked back. She was still standing there, a ghostly figure in the moonlight, watching me. Both of us at the same moment raised our hands to our lips, and then I turned and fled. I walked

sharply down the avenue until I came to within
a hundred yards of the Lodge gates; but I was
afraid of being seen or heard, so made a detour,
and scaled the old brick wall some hundred yards
to the east of it.   In a few minutes more I was
walking briskly eastwards on the high road to
London, with a certain amount of regret when I
thought of those, and the old life, I had left
behind, but with no slight degree of hope and
elation in my heart.   I was fairly launched on
the world now, and all its romance lay before
me.

CHAPTER IV.

"AN ODD ADVENTURE."

IT may seem strange to some people that I should have chosen to run away at night when the chances were I would have to walk the whole fifteen miles to London, instead of taking train through the day and journeying comfortably in half an hour right into the metropolis. Had I pursued the latter course, however, I would most assuredly have been seen and probably stopped before I got to the end of my journey, whereas, now, even if I walked, I would be in London long before I was missed and would have booked a steerage to Australia or South America before any one on the look out for me could interfere. I was not particular as to which of the two countries named I went to: I would take the first boat to either, and keep out of sight until they sailed. My main desire was to get out of the country. Never did a boy place himself more at the disposal of chance than I did.

It was a lovely night, and at first I enjoyed the walk so much that it seemed folly to hail any of the market gardeners' waggons that rattled

past, loaded up with all sorts of fruits and vegetables for Covent Garden. But my well packed
black bag, although small, soon became irksome
to carry; it was a case of shifting it too often
from one hand to the other. At Colnbrook my
boots began to hurt, and I sat down close to a
watering trough by the roadside. Before many
minutes a waggoner drove up. He had a load
of cabbages piled up so high that I wondered
they did not topple over. I asked him if he
would give me a seat on the front of the waggon
with him as far as Covent Garden, and I would
pay him for the ride. Before many minutes he
was the richer by eighteen-pence, and I was
sitting on what might be called the box seat of
the waggon. I began to feel rather sleepy
and at times dozed off; it is more than likely
I would have fallen from my seat had it
not been that the waggoner, who was a good-
natured sort of man, put his arm over my
shoulder and held me in my place. On one
occasion I must have slept for a considerable
time, for on opening my eyes, I was astonished
to find that it was broad daylight, and we were
jogging smoothly and silently over a wooden
pavement with houses on either side.

We were in London at last. Then I recognised
Holland Park and the High Street, Kensington.
A little farther on and Kensington Gardens
was on our left. How strange it was to see the
Row in the broad light of day without a single
human being in it. In Piccadilly there were a

few hansoms and carts in the roadway, but only a solitary policeman on the pavement. It was only when we came to the Strand, and approached Covent Garden that any considerable signs of life were apparent in the sleeping city.

Saying good-bye to my friend the waggoner, I took my black bag and strolled about the market watching with interest the tons upon tons of fruits, vegetables and flowers that came pouring in from the remotest parts of England and the Continent, to satisfy the needs of the greatest conglomeration of human beings on the face of the earth, and I found myself wondering what would happen if this supply were suddenly to cease. As yet it was only four o'clock in the morning, and, though the sun was beginning to show itself, I felt cold and somewhat stiff, doubtless owing to having slept on the front seat of the waggon. A good wash and a cup of coffee with something to eat appealed to my imagination very powerfully then; but as yet, so far as I knew, there were no hotels open, so I would have to make the best of things for two or three hours at least.

Wandering into a little side street, I caught sight of a coffee-stall and made straight for it. There were a few rough, furtive-eyed men who looked as if they had been up all night, loafing round it, but I did not mind that; the coffee-stall seemed cleanliness itself, the steaming urns and the bread and butter were just what my

system was craving for just then, so going up to
one end of the long wooden counter, I boldly
asked for refreshments, paid my two-pence, and
was soon enjoying them, as I had seldom
enjoyed a meal of the kind in my life. I remembered when at school turning up my nose at
exactly the same fare, and the old saying came
home to me with peculiar force that hunger was
the best sauce. While I stood, slowly eating a
second round of bread-and-butter, and drinking
another cup of hot coffee, it came rather in the
nature of a surprise to me to see a tall, countri-
fied looking man, in evening dress and loose,
unbuttoned overcoat, step up to the far corner of
the stall opposite, and order the same refreshments as I had done. But remembering that all
sorts and conditions of men in London from city
clerks to peers are not above patronising coffee-
stalls, not to speak of hot-potato or roasted-
chestnut barrows, I overcame my surprise and
lazily watched my companion. He puzzled me :
he certainly was not a man-about-town, for his
dress-clothes were obviously ill-fitting, and he
wore a bowler hat. The man himself had a
pleasant, open countenance, he was bronzed and
bearded, and I at once put him down as a
country-cousin who had run up to town on a
short visit, and who, having been out all night at
some dance or other, had come on to Covent
Garden in the early morning, as many people
do, to see the wonderful market.

So far I was right, only, as it afterwards

transpired, the country-cousin came from
Canada. I noticed that he wore a rather heavy
gold chain, and as he unconcernedly drank his
coffee, the little crowd of rough, shady-looking
youths drew up to the counter and jostled each
other against it. Suddenly, and before I had
the slightest suspicion as to their intentions, one
of them made a sudden snatch at his heavy
chain, and in another moment made off with it
and the watch.

Now, and I say it without boasting, there were
few boys at Harrow who could come near me in
doing a hundred yards, and that accomplish-
ment stood me in good stead on the present
occasion. I flung the cup from my hand, and
was after him before the others could prevent
me. Before he had gone fifty yards I had
sprung upon him, and seized the hand in which
he held the watch. He tried to throw it from him,
but I succeeded in clutching it. Then we both
rolled over together, and I was conscious that
the other roughs had come to the assistance of
their comrade, and were trying to wrest the
watch from me. But I stuck to it for all I was
worth, and tried to keep them off. Someone
kicked me on the side, and I was beginning to
feel queer, when thud, thud, and the roughs
went spinning right and left as the man who
had lost the watch came up and dispersed them
with his big fists in a way that was edifying to
witness. He had been tripped up by the thief's
confederates, which accounted for his delay in

coming to my rescue sooner. I still held on to the culprit, but I was only too glad to hand him over to the stranger, for one of the roughs had served me a cowardly trick, and all I was good for was to sit down on the stone pavement speechless, gasping for breath. But the stranger did not trouble much about the thief; with his open hand he boxed his ears in a way that made me feel thankful it was not my ears that were being boxed; then, taking him by the nape of the neck, he flung him half across the road and turned his attention to me. Without being able to speak, I handed him his watch; and then everything seemed to spin round and round about me, and I fell forward on my face. When I came to myself again, which must have been in a very few minutes, I found myself propped up against the strange gentleman's knees, while a porter stood in front of me sprinkling water on my face out of a pail.

"You'll be all right in another minute, my boy," said the stranger in a voice that sounded very friendly indeed. "Just sit quietly, until you get your breath back again."

In a few minutes more I struggled to my feet, feeling not a little stiff and dazed.

"Where are you going to?" asked the stranger, slipping his arm into mine.

"To the coffee-stall for my bag," I replied, "and then to an hotel—it doesn't much matter which one I go to."

"Then you'll come to mine and be my guest,"

said the big man in evening dress. "I'm in your debt more than I can tell you. That watch was a presentation one, and I wouldn't have lost it for five hundred pounds."

But there was no bag at the coffee-stall; the thieves had spirited it away as soon as I had started in pursuit of their mate. A horrible presentiment possessed me. I thrust my hand into the breast-pocket of my jacket, only to discover that the packet which Muriel Wray had given me was gone. The thieves had effectually relieved me of it in the scrimmage. I searched for my purse, but it had been in the same pocket as Muriel Wray's money, and I realised that I was without a penny in the world, before almost having begun my journey! Something like a groan escaped my lips. This came of helping a stranger! And what was the stranger going to do for me? Nothing, of course; if I told him, he might only think it was a scheme of mine to get money out of him. I remained silent, and leant against the coffee-stall to think. The stranger must have seen the look of blank despair upon my face, for he asked——

"What's the matter, my boy, have those chaps gone through you?"

"Yes," I replied, "for every penny I possess. I can't go with you to any hotel. I haven't even got a spare shirt to my back, they've taken my bag, too."

"And I saw them take it, but was too late to stop them. Never mind; I'll see what can be

done ; you've got to come with me. Here, boy,"
—he turned to a bare-legged urchin standing
hard by — "call a cab. You'll come to my
hotel."

In three minutes more we were sitting together in a hansom, bowling up Regent Street,
which was now beginning to show some signs
of life. The drive through the fresh morning
air seemed to put new life into me. My companion asked no questions. He merely laughingly remarked that when we got to the hotel, a
good tub would do neither of us any harm, and
a good breakfast afterwards would do us still
less. After that we could have a rest if we felt
so inclined. And then we pulled up at the
Langham.

In an hour's time we were sitting together at
a most excellent breakfast. My newly-found
friend had exchanged his evening dress for a
well-made, orthodox morning suit, and at once
I put him down as a country squire or gentleman farmer; but what puzzled me about him
was that he occasionally used a form of speech
which was quite unfamiliar to me. Once or
twice I thought I detected Americanism. Breakfast over, he asked me, in a quiet matter-of-fact
way, if I belonged to London, and what I intended doing. Now, I had been wondering
what on earth I should do, seeing that my
means of leaving the country had been so unexpectedly taken from me. Back to the Cedars
I could not possibly go—I would have broken

stones by the road-side before doing that—but what to do under the circumstances, that was the question. He looked like a man I could trust. Surely he would not give me away after what had occurred. In ten minutes he was in possession of my story.

"I thought it was something of that sort," he said, smilingly. "Of course, you can't go back to your uncle's. How much money did you lose this morning?"

I told him, remarking that, of course, I did not do so under any expectation that he would make it good.

"Look here, Derringham," he said, "you did me a good turn this morning, and you did it as pluckily as anything I ever saw done in my life, and I'm in your debt. Now, I'll give you the choice of two things. I'll either pay you back that money in full, because I know that every word you tell me is gospel truth, or I'll take you with me to Canada. My name is Dunbar—Colin Dunbar. I own a cattle and horse ranche on the Cypress Hills, in the North-West Territories, and I sail from Liverpool to-morrow with some valuable prize stock I'm taking out to the ranche.

It's a pretty wild sort of place, remember, and there are a good few Indians—mostly renegade Siouxs—knocking around, not to speak of horse-thieves and whisky smugglers, but if you care to come out to it, I'll give you a berth and look after you. I'll pay your passage out, and rig you out as well when you get there. There are two other men going out with the stock, but you can lend a hand, and that will keep you from wearying. Now what is it to be?"

" I'll go with you, sir," I exclaimed, and my heart beat fast with the thought of it

"Then here's a fiver in the meantime," he said, "you may want to buy some things. I'd advise you not to go out more than you can help. We'll leave to-night at seven for Liverpool."

CHAPTER V.

"THE UNEXPECTED HAPPENS."

THAT same evening we drove to Euston, and it must be admitted I did not breathe freely until the train was steaming out of the station. Fearful of being recognised and taken back to my uncle's, I only ventured once out of the hotel that day, and that was to go a few doors down Regent Street and buy a bag, some underclothing, and a few necessary articles for the voyage. I did not weary in the train, there was so much to think about. It was difficult to believe that it was only a matter of some twenty hours since I had left the Cedars, and said good-bye to Muriel Wray. My uncle Gilbert, despite his somewhat arbitrary action, I still looked back upon with affection, but in the girl it was as if I had left behind the one good friend who really and truly had an interest in my welfare, who would, if she knew of it, be happy in my success, and sorry to hear of my troubles. Why it should be so was to me an unaccountable thing : how any girl could care for one who only treated her as a girl, that is to say with little else than a spirit of toleration, was something that passed my understanding. I had not gone out of my way to make myself agreeable to her at any time, even although I had come to think her the prettiest girl I had ever seen in my life, and by far the nicest. It could only have been the nobility of her character that made her take such a practical interest in a penniless orphan like myself. How soured and how utterly an outcast would I have felt myself if it had not been for her sweet friendship. Oh! how I despised myself and burnt with shame on thinking of the time — and more than once — when I was ashamed to be seen walking with her, simply because she was a girl. I wondered if she had noticed it, and what she must have thought of me if she did. But she had a soul above such things, and when on one occasion my action was too obvious to avoid remark, she had merely suggested that I was shy. She would not wittingly have hurt anyone's feelings for the world. If only another opportunity presented itself of showing how much I really cared for and respected her, how different would be my behaviour. But I would write to her on my arrival in Liverpool and keep her posted as to my doings, at least so far as it was possible; this would show that I was not ungrateful. And she would write to me to the ranche; it would be something for which to look forward.

We arrived in Liverpool about midnight, and went straight to bed in the hotel. Mr. Dunbar had been very kind and considerate, speaking to me as if I had been an equal or as old as himself. There was a bluff heartiness about him that inspired confidence. Next forenoon was a busy one; we went down to the docks and got the cattle on board; being very valuable animals the greatest care had to be exercised. There were two hands, odd, nondescript-looking men, who earned a living by going backwards and forwards across the Atlantic with cattle; they managed the timid creatures with a skill that was truly wonderful, still, on one or two occasions, a suspicious Red Rose cow would deliberately sit down and prop itself up with its front feet when half way across the gangway, and refuse to budge. Then Mr. Dunbar and I would have to go behind it and push for all we were worth.

By three in the afternoon all preparations had been completed; the whistle blown warningly three or four times; the gangway withdrawn, the cables cast adrift, and the great screw had begun to revolve, causing a strange quiver throughout the ship. Then the little group on the pier seemed to swim before my eyes and recede, there were a few cheers that died away in a dispiriting fashion; a waving of hats, hands and handkerchiefs, and we were off down the Mersey. There was not a soul on that pier to bid me good-bye or God-speed, but I knew that in a certain old country house in Middlesex there was one who was doubtless thinking of

me then, and the thought was comforting. I
was glad that I had seized an opportunity of
writing to her that morning, telling of my
unexpected fortune, and giving her the address
of the nearest post town to the ranche, which
was that of Maple Creek. I felt sorry to leave
England, but, of course, not so much as other
boys would have been who were leaving father,
mother, or relatives behind. While I was
watching the receding shore and thinking
about these thing, Mr. Dunbar came up to me.

"Well, Derringham," he said, in his hearty
way, "are you wishing yourself ashore again?
If you do, it's not too late yet."

"No, sir," I replied, "there's nothing to keep
me in England. I'm only too glad to get
away."

"That's right, and if you don't like the ranche
you needn't stop there. Let's go down and get
some tea from the steward."

It would weary the reader to give an account
of my voyage in the *Cambrian* across the
Atlantic. Suffice it, that for the first three or
four days the weather was rough for the season
of the year, and most of the time I was sick.
The cattle were knocked about considerably, but
still there were no deaths among them. Despite
my sickness, I forced myself to crawl about the
pens in which they were confined, and tried to
make myself generally useful. Two or three
times the rancher, Mr. Dunbar, told me to go
and lie down, but I did not care to see the other

two men working day and night while I lay on my bunk. It is my belief that forcing oneself to keep moving, and thus distracting the mind from the ailing condition of the body, is more conducive to getting over sea-sickness quickly than anything else, although, perhaps, it may slightly aggravate the sickness for the time being. Upon the whole I enjoyed the voyage, and when we got to Halifax my appetite was simply appalling.

A few days' rest, and then we put the cattle on the cars, or, as we would say in England, the cattle trucks. Then for three days and nights we ran right on to Winnipeg, through some of the wildest and grandest scenery one could possibly imagine. The strangeness and novelty of everything was a continual source of delight. The weather was warm—almost unpleasantly warm—but I did not mind that much. I took off my coat and waistcoat in the caboose, which was the name of the large sleeping and eating van attached to the freight train by which we travelled, and when the train was shunted into the siding at some lonely section-house to let another train pass, I helped to feed and water the cattle in my shirt-sleeves, and felt as if I were at least giving some equivalent for my food and passage. The other two men were very civil to me when they found that I was anxious to help. Theirs was a strange existence indeed; I do not believe that during the entire journey they ever once took off a stitch of clothing.

When one comes to think, however, that those men had always to be ready to go at a moment's notice to the help of some valuable animal in trouble, their seemingly careless ways are not without excuse.

The great lakes were a revelation to me; it was not difficult to imagine that one looked once more upon the sea. And there were the waters and the shores which were steeped in the romantic associations of the past, where the Red Man roamed in the dark pine woods and the picturesque voyageur shot the rapids in his birch canoe. At Winnipeg we rested for twenty-four hours, and allowed the cattle to stretch themselves in a covered yard. It was difficult to believe that this large, well-laid out city of Winnipeg with its palatial hotels and magnificent buildings was only a few years before the miserable little village of Fort Garry, consisting of the fort itself and a few log, mud-daubed huts.

We walked up Main Street, and saw the old gateway of the Hudson's Bay trading post or fort. It was all that remained of that old stockaded building, the history of which is simply one long romance. Who has not read "The Great Lone Land," of Butler, in which he tells of how in 1870, Lord Wolseley, then Colonel Wolseley, when in command of what is known as the Red River Expedition, surprised the rebel and murderer, Louis Riel, within its walls. Along the banks of that Red River flowing hard-by, and not so long ago, has blood been spilt like water, and the white man, the half-breed, and the Red Man have striven for supremacy.

Next day we were once more in the train and steaming out of Winnipeg. We were now in the prairie country, and to me it was a remarkable sight. Far as the eye could reach, the country was as flat as a billiard table. There was nothing save an occasional farm-house to break the dead level—the unfettered expanse of that seemingly illimitable prairie land—not a tree, a stick, nor a stone to relieve the appalling sameness. The horizon seemed to creep up and up as the train sped along and met the sky-line. It was for all the world like being at sea. And in truth, this great prairie is nothing after all but an old ocean-bed, and almost anywhere in it, if you dig, you can find fossils of fish and shells. It stretches in a series of steppes from the Red River to the Rocky Mountains, a distance of nearly a thousand miles.

The little towns we stopped at amused me immensely. They were mostly built of wood with raised side-walks, and when a train came in, all the inhabitants in their shirt-sleeves turned out to gaze at us. The engine-driver told me it was their one excitement of the day, and principal amusement. Three more days and nights in the train, and nothing but that seemingly endless prairie, saving a few shallow lakes covered with wild-fowl. At last we arrived at our destination, Maple Creek, and heartily glad I was to find myself once more on good solid ground; and I am quite sure the cattle were just as glad as I was.

Maple Creek consisted of one little street of wooden houses and stores on the south side of the railway line, or track, as it is called in North America. It was here I saw my first cowboys, and very picturesque and strange they seemed to me, with great heavy-fringed leggings, like trousers, called chaperegos, reaching to the waist; revolver pouches in which were weapons with highly ornamented handles from ebony to mother of-pearl; buckskin shirts covered with a mosaic wrought in silk and beads, the work of some half-breed or Indian woman; great jangling Mexican spurs with rowels an inch and a half in diameter, and broad brimmed wide-a-wake hats, the like of which I had only seen in pictures. Some red-coated members of the North-West Mounted Police were on the platform, they were of a girth and stature that made me wonder how they managed to get horses strong enough to carry them. They wore the uniform of the British dragoon. I saw the fort or post gleaming white about a mile and a half from the town.

But what interested me most of all was a glimpse of rolling hills away to the south. They were the Cypress Hills, and the first ranching country of any importance in Assiniboia. After having passed over hundreds of miles of dead level, these hills were a very refreshing sight indeed. I was glad to hear that Mr. Dunbar's

ranche lay far away across them to the south-
west, beyond civilisation, in a wild uninhabited
country where one could travel for days and
days right into Montana and not see a living
soul, save predatory Indians, or horse-thieves
and murderers fleeing from justice, and of whom
it was as well to be very wary indeed. More
than one cowboy had gone out from Mr. Dunbar's ranche and never come back again. Indeed, even on the ranche a large supply of fire-
arms and ammunition, and a sharp look-out
were always kept, for occasionally large bands
of Blood, Piegan, and renegade Sioux Indians
were seen hovering about in the neighbourhood.
As yet they had never attacked the ranche
buildings, but they had several times wrought
devastation among the stock, and of late there
had been rumours of a general uprising amongst
the tribes. This had made the rancher somewhat anxious, and take extra precautions.

I found the cowboys had come to drive the
cattle to the ranche. There was also a waggon
with four horses to take out certain necessary
stores, and a couple of spare saddle horses with
a pack-horse. I was not long in finding out for
whom the latter were meant.

"You'll come on with me," said the squatter,
"the waggon will travel with the cattle. They
won't get to the ranche for four or five days at
least. If we start off now we can do twenty
miles before dark, and camp at Waller's, Grey-
burn Coullee."

A Californian saddle with a high peak was something new to me, but I had been accustomed to horses, and was considered a good rider. When we had got some ten miles from the little town, the country began to get hilly with a vengeance. We came to deep, wooded ravines called "coullees," dark, still lakes, high, steep hill-sides, and great plateaus called "benches."

It was in following up one of the pine-clad ravines that the first real adventure I ever had in my life occurred. Mr Dunbar was riding on ahead along the narrow path or trail, when *puff ! ping !* and a bullet struck the cantle of the rancher's saddle, and ricochetted into the opposite bank. It was a narrow shave if there ever was one. My companion coolly turned his horse, and came galloping back to where I was leading the pack-horse. He got behind it, and taking a short whip from the horn of his saddle cracked it vigorously behind the latter.

"Now then, Derringham," he cried, "we've got to get out of this? It's the Indians, and we haven't the ghost of a show here. On with you ! "

I dug my heels into the sides of my riding horse, but before it could gather itself together and spring forward, there was another sharp *ping !* I felt the poor brute quiver beneath me, in another moment it had sprung forward and fallen all of a heap, sending me flying over its head.

CHAPTER VI.

A DUEL TO THE DEATH.

My poor horse had been shot under me, and as I was hurled over its head the halter-shank with which the pack-horse was led, was jerked out of my hand. The shock when I came to earth was so violent that it was as if all the life had been knocked out of my body. For the moment it was difficult to realise what had happened. The first thing that brought me to my senses was the voice of the rancher shouting—

"Derringham, Derringham, get up for goodness' sake, and mount the pack; it's your only chance! It's no use staying here to be killed."

Pulling myself together I struggled to my feet and staggered towards the pack-horse. The rancher, seeing my condition, sprang from his horse, and gripped the hooks that held the pack-bags on the saddle.

"Now, up you go," cried Dunbar.

In another moment I was astride the pack-bags. Leaping into his saddle, the rancher caught up the halter-shank attached to the pack, unwound his long whip lash and cracked it vigorously. Like a bolt shot from a cross-bow my steed bounded forward.

"Hold on like grim death," cried the rancher. "It's a bit rough on you, but better to feel a little sore afterwards than be scalped by those wretches."

Ping! ping! and a couple of shots rang out from unseen depths as we simply tore at breakneck speed up the ravine, between the dense, dark walls of undergrowth and pines. *Whiz, whiz, zip!* and a couple of bullets passed unpleasantly close to our heads and buried themselves with an ominous, hollow sound in the trunks of the opposite pines.

How I stuck on the back of that pack-horse is a mystery to me now. Indeed, it could hardly be said that I was on its back, for I was perched like a monkey on top of the bulgy leather bags and blankets, where every motion of the animal was intensified four-fold. Fortunately, I had always been fond of riding, and to indulge my venturesome nature I had stolen many a time down to the meadows, where my uncle generally had two or three horses on the grass, and mounting one of them, without saddle or bridle, had galloped like a circus-rider round and round the paddock. Bad spills never seemed to daunt me, I do not think anything short of having my neck broken would have done so. How those mad predilections stood me in good stead now!

"If one could only get those cowardly brutes out into the open," cried Colin Dunbar, "there would be no occasion to run like this. But revolvers are of no use against Indians in ambush with rifles, and, besides, we want to live to get back at them. Well done, Derringham, hold on!"

Whiz, zip! and a bullet struck a rock right alongside my horse ; it flattened against it and sputtered off, causing the frightened animal to leap suddenly to one side. I felt myself going, but clung to the pack with the frenzy of despair. If a strap snapped it would be all up with me, and the chances were my neck would be broken.

"Hold on," cried the rancher, "we'll be out of this in two minutes more."

By an effort I hardly thought myself capable of, I recovered my seat, and away we dashed again up that narrow ravine. How its sides echoed with the devil's tattoo our horses' feet beat on the flinty water-course ! The trees and rocks seemed to fly past at lightning speed ; it was a wild, mad ride, but it was a ride for life, for we did not know how many Indians were concealed in that lonely spot. At any moment a bullet might send one of us to our last account.

In another quarter of a mile we rounded the shoulder of a rocky ridge, and found ourselves at the bottom of a rather steep incline leading to the summit. Seeing we were now out of the zone of fire, and that it was rather hard upon the already reeking and overtaxed pack-horse to climb it with me on its back, I jumped off with the intention of walking alongside.

"That's right," remarked the rancher, as he drew rein, "a merciful man is merciful to his beast. Hilloa! what's that over there in that little hollow across the coullee?"

I looked in the direction indicated, but could see nothing; Mr. Dunbar being on horseback, and having sharper eyes, had seen something very like horses' heads in a little dip on the other side of the valley.

"It's the Indians' horses," he exclaimed, with a pleased look on his face. "They've hidden them there, but I'll reckon we'll turn the tables on 'em yet. If we can only get these horses away, we can send a messenger into the fort from Waller's ranche and have the Mounted Police out by to-morrow morning. If we have Waller's men stationed on the plateau to-night they'll not dare to leave the valley. Luckily it's full moon. Just freeze on to this pack-horse until I go and have a look at their horses."

He drew a large size Colt's revolver from its pouch as he spoke, and wheeled his horse so as to cut off through the undergrowth; for at this point the pines had ceased, and in their place there was only a straggling tangle of wild raspberries and gooseberries breast high.

"Then look out," I cried, "and don't go straight on to them. I'm almost certain I saw

the head of an Indian above the bank just
now."

As it turned out, the plumed head and long
black snaky locks that for a moment appeared
to bob up over the ridge, was not the creature
of my heated imagination, but a stern fact.

"All right, Derringham," cried the rancher,
airily, "if anything happens to me, just you mount
the pack again, give it its head, and follow up
the trail ; you'll come to Waller's ranche in less
than half an hour. We've got to teach those
chaps a lesson somehow."

He put spurs to the splendid animal he rode,
and dashed into the undergrowth, revolver in
hand. Colin Dunbar was a splendid specimen
of humanity, and sat his horse as if he were part
of it. I ascended the hill-side so as to have a
bettter view of what happened. Until now I
had not been particularly frightened, the shooting and our head-long race had followed so
quickly upon each other that there had been no
time to think of consequences. But, now that I
had to remain passive while my friend, the
rancher, rode on to what might be a death trap,
my heart grew sick with a strange dread, and
my limbs trembled with suppressed excitement.
Oh, if I could only have had a revolver and
been by his side to second him, there would
have been little of fear in my heart! As it was,
my part was only to watch and wait.

But not for long. The rancher, fortunately
for him, did not ride straight into the hollow

where the horses were. Had he done so he would have been a dead man. He galloped his horse through the undergrowth until he was abreast of it, and I saw his intention was to slightly ascend the opposite hill-side and then descend. It was quite evident he knew what he was doing, and that it was not the first time he had fought Indians. He was not to have it all his own way, however, for he had hardly begun to ascend when *puff, ping!* and Dunbar's hat went flying into the air, spinning round and round like a plate manipulated by the stick of a Japanese juggler. It was as close a call as ever I saw in my life. Then there was as smart a piece of action, both on the rancher's and on the Indian's part, as one could wish to see.

It was an incongruous idea, but for all the world it put me in mind of the manœuvres of two antagonists in a polo match. Dunbar's blood was up. He wheeled his horse and rode down upon the Indian in the hollow at full gallop, revolver in hand, but the Indian was too quick for him. I saw the latter, still grasping his smoking rifle, turn round, seize a horse by the mane, and leap on its back with the agility of a circus-rider. The next moment the Indian's shaggy, wiry-limbed pony was climbing up the steep hill-side like a jack-rabbit. The rancher bent forward over the horse's neck, steadying himself by grasping a lock of his horse's mane firmly in his left hand, and cut off at an angle to intercept him. When within a few yards of him

5

Colin Dunbar levelled his revolver and fired, but it would have been little less than chance work had he hit the Indian, seeing that the pace of the two horses was only a succession of laboured leaps.   It was quite evident the rancher had missed his mark.   Knowing that the latter was overtaking him, the Indian suddenly changed his tactics, turned his horse in its own length, and bounded along the hill-side in a lateral direction.

The rancher did not turn so easily, and I feared the Indian would escape.   But the latter, in his excitement, had evidently forgotten his bearings, for on getting to the little clear space at the bottom of the valley, he essayed to ride right up it on to the plateau, but was confronted by the dense tangle of undergrowth.   Right bravely he endeavoured to charge and force his way through, but it was too much for him; apprehensive of being caught like a rat in a trap, he reared his horse and in a couple of leaps was clear of it again.   For a moment he hesitated. Then, catching sight of the upward trail, he turned his horse's head towards it.   I was partly hidden by a little clump of saskatoon bushes, and in all probability in his excitement he had forgotten my presence.   Up the steep trail he came towards me, bending low over his horse's neck.   A picturesque figure he was truly, clad in loose shirt and leggings of red flannel, covered with glowing bead-work of red, yellow and blue, and with white ermine tails streaming from his arms, breast and legs. A great plume stood upright amid his long, black, braided locks, and even at a distance of sixty yards I could see his black eyes glowing with a baleful light. He guided his steed in a most ingenious fashion, with a single rein attached to its lower lip; in all probability he also used his hands and feet.

I had to turn that Indian if he rode me down. Picking up a couple of stones about the shape and size of a cricket ball, I waited for his approach. On he came, and then, when he was within about ten yards of me, I stepped out right in front of him on to the trail. He sat up on his horse's back as if in surprise when he saw me. Now was my opportunity. With all the strength that was in me I hurled a stone at him as one would deliver an overhand ball on the cricket field. It struck him full on the breast, and for a moment he swayed in the saddle. I had drawn the pack-horse across the trail so as to block his progress. Quick as thought I seized my second stone and hurled it as before. But I missed him this time, striking his plucky little horse instead; the latter, scared by the sudden and unexpected appearance of such hostile obstacles, and before the Indian could prevent it, turned right round and bolted down the trail again.

Now was the rancher's chance. His horse had missed its footing just as it reached the foot of the valley, and had come down with him, fortunately on good, soft turf. He had the presence of mind to throw the revolver from him as he fell. He was unhurt, but to pick up the revolver and remount had caused a delay of a few moments. Now I witnessed as exciting a scene as ever it was my lot to behold. The Indian charged Dunbar at full speed on the grassy bottom, although he might have escaped down the trail in the direction in which he had come. The rancher checked his horse and warily watched his approach, revolver in hand.

The Indian, who had not been able to reload, seized his rifle by the barrel and came on swinging it round his head. The rancher waited until he was within five yards, and fired point-blank in his face. But the bullet struck the stock of the whirling rifle, and before he had time to fire a second shot, the Indian was in upon him, and had aimed a terrific blow at his head. The rancher promptly ducked, and then the next thing that I saw was the two antagonists swaying together in their saddles, wrestling as only men wrestle when they are doing it for their lives. My heart was in my mouth, but they were too far off for me to render any assistance to my friend; the duel would be decided one way or another before I could possibly reach them. Their horses drew apart; they were dragged from their saddles and fell to earth, the rancher on top. Then I saw Colin Dunbar release his hold on the Indian, run a few yards to the right, and pick up the revolver which had fallen from his hand when they had been wrestling. The Indian sprang nimbly to his feet, drew a long, glittering knife from its sheath on his belt, and darted in upon the rancher. But although quick he was not quick enough, for before he could strike home Colin Dunbar levelled his revolver and fired, and the Indian fell dead at his feet.

CHAPTER VII.

THE MOUNTED POLICE ARRIVE.

ALTHOUGH the rancher's adventure with the Indian takes some little time to tell in detail, it all happened in a very few minutes. Doubtless, the other Indians down the valley, on hearing the firing, hurried up to find out whether or not their comrade had made a lucky shot. What they discovered could not have been at all to the liking of these would-be murderers, for when the Indian fell before the revolver of Colin Dunbar, I rushed down the trail in order to help him to secure their horses. I caught the dead Indian's horse—or pony, as it would be called by the Indians themselves—and then secured the rancher's. He mounted his horse immediately as if nothing particular had happened, and said—

"Now then, Derringham, I'd advise you to take that mare to the other side, and try to improvise a pair of reins while I tie these other horses together. We'll drive them in front of us; they'll follow our pack-horse along the trail.

You'll find riding that pony easier than sitting on top of the bags. Hurry up, my son!"

He galloped off to where the Indians' horses were concealed in the hollow. I leapt on the back of my new steed, and made for the place where I had left the pack. The Indian's saddle was one of the queerest things of the kind I ever saw in my life. It was very low and flat, and thickly studded with brass-headed nails. The stirrup-leathers were so ridiculously short that I considered it better to dispense with them altogether. Almost before my arrangements were completed there was a drumming of hoofs behind me, and the rancher appeared on the scene, driving in front of him two Indian ponies with saddles on their backs.

"Just tie that halter-shank round the neck of the pack," he cried, "and let it take the lead. You stay behind with me, and we'll send 'em along in front of us. On to your broncho again!—fair exchange is no robbery. You took the Indian's middle stump with that first ball of yours, but your second was a bit of a wide. Let's get a rustle on."

And away we went again at a gallop, driving the three horses before us; our pack-horse, as Mr. Dunbar had said it would, taking the lead. In a few minutes more we were out of the valley, and to my surprise I found that we were on a far-stretching plateau, or bench, as it is called in North America. It was as flat as a pancake; there was not a stick or a stone to interfere with the sense of weird desolation and solitude that the unbroken horizon line conveyed, where it stood out sharply against the evening sky. There was a glorious blood-red sunset, and the trail that opened out ahead of us, straight as an arrow, seemed to lead right into that cloud-world of crimson and gold.

Crack! went the rancher's stock-whip like the report of a pistol, and the pack-horse, as if it really enjoyed leading such an odd procession, kicked out with its hind legs and tore along the trail like a thing possessed, the Indians' horses following, and the rancher and myself bringing up the rear.

"We'll soon be at Waller's at this rate," remarked Dunbar to me, as we rode side by side; "but there's more work for us this night. Someone must ride into the fort and fetch out the Mounted Police. These Indians must be captured. I wouldn't have believed it possible that they would try their games on so near to civilisation. Had we been at the ranche, now, I wouldn't have been surprised in the very least. They must be particularly bad Indians; I fancy by their shooting and horses that there are only two of them. It was lucky for you, it was only your horse that got shot that time."

"And it was lucky for you that you weren't an inch taller that time you lost your hat," I rejoined. For despite the fact that I realised how nearly the incident was allied to tragedy, there was something grotesque in seeing a man's hat go skimming into the air without any apparent cause.

The rancher raised a hand and stroked his bare head.

"By jove, I'd quite forgotten I had lost my hat!" he remarked surprisedly. "But here's the dip leading to Waller's ranche; we'll head the horses to the corral—that's the word we use out here, by the way, for a cattle or horse-yard. Steady there!"

And to my surprise, a valley with a wide grassy bottom suddenly opened almost at our feet. In three minutes more our horses were standing panting in the middle of a large yard. Forming the four sides of a square were a number of long, low, log-huts with sod roofs. Outside them again, on the left, were two or three long ricks of hay, while in front of what I took to be the dwelling-house was a solitary clump of tall, shady, cotton-wood trees. Hard-by was a wimpling creek, and on either side the brown hill-sides, covered with all sorts of wild berries, rose up towards the bench or plateau. It was the first ranche I had ever seen, and to me it seemed very snug and picturesque.

As soon as we entered the yard four or five rough-looking men came out of one of the long low huts. They had evidently just finished their evening meal. They were, indeed, a picturesque-looking lot, and typical cowboys, their chief characteristics being a superfluity of long hair, and a weakness for chaperegos—

leather overalls—huge spurs and revolvers. I sometimes wondered if they went to bed wearing the latter, for I do not remember ever having seen a cowboy without such articles. One of these men was Waller himself, but he was hardly distinguishable from the others. It was only on looking into his dark thoughtful eyes that one saw the gulf that brains and energy fixed between their possessor and his less favoured fellows. He had made a home for himself out of the wilderness, and owned a tract of land as large as an English county. In as few words as possible, Dunbar gave an account of what had occurred. Waller turned to one who seemed to be the youngest of the cov. boys, and said—

"I say, Billie, you just saddle up and ride to the fort as slippy as you like, and tell 'em about this affair. Michelle, you saddle up, too, and go to the lower end of the valley. Don't let any one enter or leave it. Pete, you stay at the top end. Both of you look out for yerselves, and don't go too near cover unless you want an ounce or two of lead introduced into your systems. Dunbar, after you've had something to eat, you can have a fresh horse, and we'll take opposite sides of the coullee. If we can only keep them Indians there till the Mounted Police come up in the morning, it is just possible we may be able to take them alive. Anyhow, it's pretty certain there'll be a high old time."

In less than half-an-hour the rancher's wife was giving us a most substantial supper. There were tender and juicy bear-steaks, a little rich perhaps, but not too much so for men who had been in the saddle for the greater part of the day; boiled eggs, beautiful butter, rich cream; the green tea so much used in North America, pleasant enough when one grows accustomed to it; fresh home-made bread, honey, cranberry jelly, and to finish up with, pancakes and maple syrup It was a supper fit for an emperor, and the fresh dry air, and the ride, enabled me to do it full justice. I was glad to think that the Canadians knew how to live.

After supper we saddled up, for I had prevailed upon the rancher to allow me to accompany them. At first they had negatived my request to make one of the party, Mr. Dunbar declaring that I had undergone risks enough for one day without tempting Providence further. He had advised me to retire early and have a good night's rest; as for himself and the others, they were accustomed and hardened to such like experiences. I, however, doubtless showed my disappointment so plainly that the rancher let me come.

"Well, look here, Derringham, I feel a certain amount of responsibility in regard to you, just as much, indeed, as if you had been given into my charge. Had anything happened to you to-day, I would never have forgiven myself taking you out here. I would much rather you stayed away, but if you are bent upon coming I suppose you must come. But you'll have to obey me ; and recollect, I'm not going to let you run any more risks than I can help."

I recognised and appreciated the spirit in which he spoke, so readily agreed to do as he desired. In half-an-hour I was mounted on a good, fresh horse, and we were cantering along the trail towards the wooded valley. The moon was full, and so clear the night, that with five people on the patrol it would be difficult for the Indians to pass out unobserved. We rightly concluded that they would not try to do so until about daybreak, when, having observed us patrolling the valley all night, they naturally supposed our vigilance would be somewhat relaxed through drowsiness.

Arrived at the scene of action, Waller—the rancher—separated from Mr. Dunbar and myself; each party taking opposite sides. We kept well out in the open, as otherwise it might have been a very easy matter for the Indians to have picked us out with their rifles, under cover of the bank in the clear moonlight.

The night wore on, and it was as much as I could do to prevent myself going to sleep in the saddle. For the first time I realised that I could not stand the same fatigue and go so many hours without sleep as those who were so much older than myself, and whose lives were one long course of training. The rancher hardly spoke at all, but occasionally drew out his pipe and smoked. It began to grow cold, and I was glad to have taken his advice and put on an overcoat.

Truly there was nothing like experience in such matters after all. It grew darker, and then the stars began to go out one by one, like lights in a great city at break of day. Suddenly, in the death-like stillness, there echoed out one of the most unearthly howls it was ever my lot to listen to, but the rancher told me it was only a coyote or timber wolf.

My thoughts were straying again, and I was nodding in the saddle, when suddenly a prolonged whistle shrilled out from the opposite side of the valley, and immediately following it the sharp ring of a rifle. In another second there were two other shots. In the grey dawnlight we could see the cause of the commotion. The two Indians, on seeing Waller pass, had thought to make a run for it and escape from the valley unseen. But the unexpected had happened, as it generally does, for Waller, looking round, had caught sight of them. He was blowing his whistle for assistance when one of the Indians drew a lead on him and fired. The bullet whizzed unpleasantly close to Waller's head, and the latter, forgetting that it was desirous, for the sake of making an example, to take these Indians alive, grew wroth, and promptly fired two shots from his Winchester at them as they scuttled back to cover. His shots evidently did not take effect.

"They are in the coullee, anyhow," remarked Dunbar, "and that is satisfactory. I wonder if one of them can possibly be Make-Thunder?"

" Who is he ? " I inquired.

" A bad Indian," replied the squatter; " he used to be the terror of the Saskatchewan district; he shot a policeman who tried to arrest him in the spring, and, knowing that his capture means death, he swears he will kill at least half-a-dozen before he is taken. " I'm afraid though that he'll not see the scaffold; he'll either be shot or shoot himself. It can't be long now before the Mounted Police come up. They'll soon make short work of him; it's their trade."

A streak of luminous greyish-green showed itself in the east. It stretched itself along the flat horizon-line of the plateau, and crept upwards into the heavens. It became clearer, and a sickly, wan, dawn-light took its place. Then a pale lemon-glow struggled into the eastern sky; a little bird awoke among the pine boughs in the valley and called sleepily to its mate, then another awoke, and another, and another, until there was a glorious burst of song. The lemon-glow changed to tawny yellow, the yellow to pink, and then the sun peeped over the edge of the plateau like an orb of burnished gold, and the dew sparkled on the grass as if a shower of fine diamonds had fallen during the night. Another day had dawned in that great lone prairie-land.

Suddenly Mr. Dunbar sang out——

" Hurrah! Derringham, here they come, the Riders of the Plains—the North-West Mounted Police. " Look! they are coming up in sections on each side of the valley, and posting a man here and there."

I looked, and surely enough two bodies of horsemen were approaching at a canter. In five minutes more a little body of ten Mounted Policemen and two Indian scouts had halted hard by, and an officer·came forward to speak to Mr. Dunbar. These policemen looked for all the world like dragoons, only they wore the more sensible and picturesque broad-brimmed felt hat of the cowboy. I never had seen men so magnificently mounted. They carried Winchester repeating-rifles at "the carry." Round their waists were cartridge belts filled with gleaming brass cartridges, rifle and revolver. On these same belts, and at the left side, were slung Enfield revolvers. Across their breasts were bandoliers, also full of cartridges. Their brown, kharkee coats were relieved by a neat brass regimental button; blue riding breeches with a yellow stripe, and long riding boots, reaching to the knee, completed their picturesque costumes. They were a bronzed, soldierly, wiry-looking lot, as smart a set of men as one could wish to see.

"A couple of the detachments happened to have arrived at the fort for special duty," remarked the officer after some conversation with the rancher, "and as I knew that Make-Thunder was in the neighbourhood, and I wasn't exactly sure how many Indians were on this job, I thought I'd give them all a little trip.

We'll surround the valley and close in upon them on foot. I'd like to take Make-Thunder alive if I can. I've left a mounted man here and there, so we'll picket out the rest of the horses, and begin at once." He turned towards his men——

"Squad, 'tion! Prepare to dismount," he cried.

CHAPTER VIII.

THE ESCAPE OF MAKE-THUNDER.

THE horses were picketed at intervals, and two men left in charge. Then the officer, who was an inspector and bore the rank of captain, addressed the troops and gave them his instructions. It was to the effect that every man was to observe the greatest caution, and not to expose himself rashly, as the Indians, being desperate, would in all probability fight to the bitter end. At the same time, as he had told Mr. Dunbar, he wanted to take them alive if possible. The party would spread out and descend the valley, at the mouth of which were four mounted men. He then gave them orders to extend.

I did not understand till afterwards why he found it necessary to warn his men against being over zealous. It seemed that these Mounted Policemen were such dare-devils, and took such a pride in the efficiency of the force to which they belonged, and its unparalleled reputation for bravery, that they were continually running the greatest risks.

6

Mr. Dunbar would not hear of me going on foot with the troopers and scouring the pine-wood. I begged of him to let me go with himself and the officer, and promised to keep well in the background; but he was obdurate, and told me to proceed with my horse to the head of the valley where I could look down it and see all that was going on. Remembering my promise of obedience on the previous night, I at once obeyed. Then the men spread out in the form of a horse-shoe on either side of the valley, and began to close in upon it. Arrived at the brink they cautiously looked around and began to descend. I followed up, and ensconced myself in the shadow of a little clump of choke-cherry bushes, where I could see right down the rugged pine-clad ravine. Some of the men would have pretty stiff climbing to do to keep in line. Indeed, I wondered if it were not possible for the moccasined Indians to scale one of those precipitous rocks and hide in some hole or crevasse until the Mounted Police had passed, and then endeavour to make good their escape. But there were still one or two mounted men stationed at intervals on the brink of the valley, and they surely would be more than a match for Indians on foot.

The first thing I saw on looking down the grassy bottom, and not more than two hundred yards from where I stood, was the dead body of the Indian who had so nearly killed my friend, the rancher, on the previous day. I noticed that

the body lay face downwards with hands out-
stretched; the sight made me shudder, there
was something about it so rigid, so uncanny.
The inspector went down and glanced at it
hastily; Mr. Dunbar would not, however, as
much as look upon his late foe. Despite his
bluff, brusque ways he was in reality one of the
most tender-hearted men I ever met.

In a few minutes the searchers were lost sight
of in the thick scrub. No one was allowed to
travel down the trail as there they might prove
an easy mark to the Indians. Ten minutes
passed and there was not a sound from the
valley, only once or twice I saw a policeman
climbing like a cat to skirt the steep face of a
ledge of rocks so as to have a good look around.
It seemed to me that this appeared very like
taking chances on one's life. There was one
tall, almost precipitous peak, which resembled a
sugar-loaf, on the south side of the ravine, with
an odd split at the top as if some Titan had
hacked it with a mammoth knife. At the foot
of it, where no pines grew, I observed a policeman and Indian scout. They looked upwards,
but, naturally enough, deeming that even a
Rocky Mountain sheep could not climb such a
formidable wall of rock, they passed on and were
soon lost sight of in the pine wood.

Whether it was from the want of sleep, or the
excitement of the previous day, I cannot tell,
but I found my mind drifting from the present
with its stern surroundings and gliding into a by

no means unpleasant series of day-dreams. There was one dream or picture that captivated my fancy immensely, and which stood out in the mirror of the mind with a realistic force that was almost as convincing as actuality. It was that of Muriel Wray, and I thought I could see her as on one occasion she had sat in the old summer-house, looking out into the dim depths of the pine wood, a stray shaft of sunlight creating a glory in the silky mazes of her hair. Until I had met her I had hardly thought a girl worth speaking to. Yes, she was something like a girl—a sweet-tempered, big-hearted, glorious girl. I believe she would have lived on bread-and-water for a week rather than unwittingly hurt the feelings of the veriest waif. I knew she often denied herself things she had set her heart on, to relieve the needs of others. I thought of the twenty pounds she had lent me, and wondered how long it would be before I was able to pay her back again.

*   *   *   *

Ping! Ping! Ping! and my dream shivered as the sharp ring of rifles broke on the stillness. *Ping! Ping!* again and again, and the ravine rang with horrible echoes. From a little knoll half-way down the valley, and close to an over-hanging cliff with an open space all round, I could see little jets of flame spurt, and then wreaths of smoke rise, floating lazily into the sunlit air. Then from certain points among the pines came more pale-blue columns sagging among the tree-tops. It was evident that the Indians had been discovered behind that little knoll under the overhanging cliff, and had opened fire on the police. It was a point of vantage from which deadly execution could be done. To rush it would be certain death to many. It would be an easier and better way to wait and starve them out, they could not possibly make their escape. And now the police had formed up in a complete half-circle, but as yet no attempt was made to rush the enemy's position.

The Indians had not even been sighted, for their natural little fort was fringed with thick masses of sage bush, and from behind it they could see without being seen. From where I was I saw that the other men, who had been stationed at various points of the valley, came hurrying up, seeing that, now the Indians were located, perhaps they would have a chance of rushing them with the others. I noticed that even one of the men in charge of the long line of picketed horses had, contrary to his orders, left his post and sneaked away to the edge of the ravine to have a good look at what was going on. If the officer, or any of the non-commissioned officers, saw him he stood a very good chance of being put under arrest for neglect of duty, and a breach of discipline.

My first impulse was to rush down the valley and join the others, but I remembered Mr.

Dunbar's injunctions, and thought it would be but a poor return for all his goodness to disregard them now. To break an order one has agreed to observe, is not only dishonourable in the extreme, but a direct insult to those in authority. And, perhaps, we can seldom guess at the pain such an action may occasion others.

It was indeed a lucky thing for me that I remained at my post, for had I gone down the trail just then under that tall pinacle of rock, the chances are I would have experienced a surprise fraught with dire results. As my eyes happen to wander towards the rock in question, to my surprise, I saw an Indian skirt its base and leisurely make for the pines on the up-side of the valley to where the horses were picketed; he carried a rifle at the trail. My first impulse was to raise an alarm, thinking he was one of the pursued Indians making good his escape, but then I remembered there were only two of them who were now hemmed in, and that the Mounted Police had brought with them two Indian scouts. Of course, this was one of them going back to the horses, probably to carry some message into the fort. How nearly I had been to making a fool of myself in my thoughtlessness and excess of zeal But what were the police going to do about the Indians? Were they going to rush them or starve them out? Then my eyes wandered from the scene of action to the obelisk-shaped rock, with the odd split on the top, and from it to the brink of the valley.

Suddenly I saw something that startled me considerably, and filled me with puzzled conjecture. The Indian, who had rounded the rock a few minutes before, had reached the top of the valley, and, crouching, was warily scanning the plateau. Being clad in sober, dun-coloured shirt and legging, probably buckskin, just as the Police scouts were, it was only by the merest accident that my eyes had detected him. Why should he observe such extraordinary precautions, seeing there was no earthly necessity for him to do so; but the man was an Indian scout and could, doubtless, no more help himself behaving in such a fashion than an actor can bring himself to believe he is not walking the boards when in private life. A desultory fire was being kept up down the valley so as to tempt the Indians to exhaust their store of ammunition. The Indian scout had now stepped boldly on to the plateau, and was walking leisurely towards the horses. The remaining policeman left in charge of them was at the far end of the line driving in a picket-pin with a wooden mallet.

It seemed to me that the scout looked up and down the long line, as if to find some particular animal. He was looking for the best horse there, but I did not know it at the time. He went over towards the sergeant-major's short-backed, bony, spirited broncho with powerful hind-quarters, the sort of animal that looked "a stayer." The sergeant-major was evidently going back to the fort to take charge, and the

officer was remaining in command; the scout
had evidently been sent to fetch the horse. Suddenly I observed that the trooper, who had been
driving in the picket-pin, had finished his work
and turned to come back down the row of horses
again. At first he did not seem to take any
particular notice of the Indian, but as his eyes
rested on him he suddenly came to a dead stop,
and the mallet dropped from his hand. Then he
shouted at the top of his voice, and ran to the
nearest horse. What on earth was the matter?
For a moment I hardly realised the situation.
Then the truth flashed upon me: the supposed
Indian scout was no other than one of the
Indians who had somehow made his escape, and
having seen the scouts from some point of vantage was trying to pass himself off as one of
them !

At the same moment as the Indian ran
towards the sergeant-major's horse, I fired six
shots out of my revolver so as to attract the
attention of the others down the valley, and
galloped off so as to frustrate, if possible, the
obvious designs of the Indian. But he was too
quick for us, for with his sharp jack-knife he cut
the leather strap of the picket rope attached to
the horse's leg, caught up the reins, flung himself into the saddle, and with a wild whoop of
triumph, was off like the wind westward. He
had taken Fandango, the best and swiftest horse
in the whole troop, there was not one left that
could even keep him in sight. But I did not

know this, and, trusting to luck, made straight
for him. By the time he had cut the picket strap
there was not sixty yards between us. The
Indian still stuck to his rifle. Doubtless, being
afraid of startling his horse he did not fire at me
before mounting. Had he done so he could have
killed me easily. He waited until he was
tearing off at full gallop, then, turning in his
saddle with an ease and agility that spoke of
long practice, he levelled his rifle at me and
fired. The bullet whizzed past my head. The
trooper had worse luck; his horse, contrary to
the habit of bronchos, put its foot in a badger-
hole, stumbled, and threw its rider heavily.
Fortunately no bones were broken.

I followed the Indian, who easily outdistanced
me, to the brink of a steep and dangerous valley.
It had been my intention to keep him in sight,
but when he tore down it, leapt the creek in the
rocky bottom, bounded up the opposite bank,
and disappeared over a ridge, I knew I had
followed in vain. When the four policemen,
who had been told off to follow, came up, I
pointed out the direction in which the fugitive
had gone, and they went off in pursuit. They
stopped out two days and nights without food,
and rode right into Montana, but they came
back to Waller's ranche with knocked-up horses,
and the sergeant-major's steed as well, to report
that they had stuck to the Indian's trail over the
wildest and roughest country imaginable, until,
on the edge of a great pine forest, they had found

poor Fandango standing dead beat, but otherwise unhurt. It was impossible to follow farther, so they had returned. The policeman who was thrown had recognised the Indian as Make-Thunder, one of the most daring and dangerous Indians in the Territories. His name was a terror to outlying settlers until at last he was brought to book—but of that, anon.

When I rode back to the valley I found the two policemen very wide-awake indeed, looking after their diminished band of picketed horses. One of them at least was liable to get into trouble, but I was not going to say anything about him if I could help it. As yet the officer very properly would not let his men rush the knoll although they were simply dying to do so. But in the course of the afternoon he gave the order, and with a wild rush the men swarmed up the steep incline. But to their great surprise they did not meet with the slightest resistance. What was the matter? When they closed in, stood on the brink of the little dip, and looked down into it, they were amazed to find only one Indian sitting calmly on the ground smoking with that stolid indifference which is peculiar to the red man. On the ground lay his rifle, and the reason of his inactivity he coolly explained to one of the Indian scouts when questioned, by saying in the Cree language that he had unfortunately, without knowing it, expended his last cartridge. His rifle was a Winchester repeater that he had stolen, which accounted for the police imagining there were two Indians behind the knoll. He also volunteered the information that Make-Thunder and he had thought it best to separate, and that the former climbed what the scouts had considered the unscaleable column of rock and lay flat in the cloven peak until the police had passed. The prisoner and would-be murderer actually held out his hands for the gleaming handcuffs to be put on his wrists. Such are some of the strange ways of the red man.

All this, however, was only a foretaste of some of the adventures yet in store for me.

CHAPTER IX.

THE PRIMEVAL WILDERNESS.

THE Indian prisoner, who bore the strange and rather inappropriate name of Young-Man-afraid-of-the-rain, admitted he had fired upon the rancher and myself on the previous day, but would not say why he had done so. In all probability he could not; a red-skin goes on the war-path for the same reason that a tiger with a taste for blood goes man-hunting. On seeing that the police had captured their man, I rode down the trail and met Mr. Dunbar at the place where my horse had been killed. I had very little pity in my heart for the captured Indian on looking upon the poor brute done to death for no reason whatever save to gratify the lust for blood and hate. I am not ashamed to say the tears came into my eyes when I helped to remove the saddle and bridle; the bullet that killed it had doubtless been meant for me, and even to the beast of burden God-given life is sweet. I would not care to be the man who makes that life a burden also.

We went back with Waller to the ranch. The inspector and a sergeant of police came with us ; the others made a camp in the valley, and before we left, a light spring waggon belonging to the police, with four splendid horses in it, had driven up, and a much-needed and substantial meal was under way. What splendid, jolly, gentlemanly fellows those policemen were! They seemed to enjoy every moment of their adventurous, out-door lives. I was almost sorry I was neither old nor big enough to become one myself. But I could not afford to spend my years in a police force, however fascinating the life might be ; I had to make my way in the world, and prove that there was the makings of a man in my composition. After the pleasant and much-needed meal which Mrs. Waller prepared for us at the ranche, my curiosity was much aroused by a conversation that took place between the inspector of police and Mr. Dunbar. The others had left the room, and on the officer looking significantly at me, my employer had simply remarked that it was all right, I was going to stay at the ranche ; he knew I was to be trusted. Whereupon the inspector seemed satisfied.

"We'll have to do something, and that very soon," the inspector observed, "this smuggled whiskey is simply flooding the country, and when the Indians get a hold of it, it simply makes them mad, and leads to crime. It even reaches them upon their reservations, and the Indian Department is blaming the police because they can't keep it out. I know it comes in on the railway, but I also know that by far the greater quantity of it is smuggled in by waggons and pack-horses from Montana over the American boundary line. I fancy a good deal of it comes across your country; you see, it's so wild and broken, and there are so many hiding-places in those great valleys and forests. We can't put out-posts everywhere when we've got a country bigger than Europe to look after, and only a thousand men. If we tried to remove them from any other place there would be an outcry at once. No, I'm afraid all we can do in the matter is to send out an occasional patrol. Besides, the Indians are causing us considerable anxiety these days. Between ourselves I wouldn't be surprised to see a general outbreak; the French half-breeds are not to be trusted, the Crees are behaving strangely, as you have just seen, and if once the Black-feet rose, well, they would make a clean sweep of the country, police and all!"

"I hardly realised it till I came to Winnipeg," said the squatter, "and what I heard there rather astonished me. Of course, a rebellion is one of those things that spreads like wild-fire." He turned to me, "I say, Derringham, I came pretty near to leaving you behind in Winnipeg, and sending you back to England again or wherever else you cared to go. You've heard what the inspector has said, and you've had a little specimen yesterday and to-day of what is likely to occur again at any time. Don't you think you'd better go back?"

"It's very good of you, sir, to give me the chance," I replied, "but with your permission I'm not going back; it's something I couldn't do. Besides, it wouldn't be fair to throw up the life before I'd given it a trial. I'm certain I'll like it. When you find me lazy or afraid of work you can pack me off at once. And as for being afraid of the Indians, we all run the same risks, and I'm quite willing to accept my share of them."

It was quite a speech for me to make, and somewhat conventional, but I meant it, every word.

"All right then, Derringham, I'll be glad to have you with me, but at the same time I feel, in a sense, responsible for you."

"Who to?" I asked, surprisedly.

"Well, I don't quite know," he answered, laughingly, with that twinkle in his eyes which betokened the humour of the man, and stroking his long, black beard, "if you were a little older I'd certainly say there was someone. Come now, isn't there someone?"

Of course, I naturally enough thought of my uncle, but somehow the rancher's query did not seem to apply in his case. My poor uncle was already too much under the thumb of his wife to have any will of his own, and I knew perfectly well by this time the latter had convinced him that I was an out-and-out bad lot, and that they were all well rid of me. No, the rancher did not

owe any responsibility to my uncle. I hardly
knew why Muriel Wray should have come into
my thoughts just then, but she did come, which
was very stupid on my part allowing her to, for,
of course, how could a man like the rancher be
responsible to a mere girl in any case! Why
the blood should have mounted into my face
just then is beyond my comprehension. I was
terribly angry with myself afterwards when I
thought that my only acknowledgment of Mr.
Dunbar's query was to shake my head with un-
called-for vigour and look foolish. I also thought
it very silly on the part of the two men to laugh—
goodness knows what there was funny to laugh at.
But the rancher desisted when he saw the indignation on my face, and in a kindly fashion said—

" Now, Derringham, I'd advise you, like a good
fellow, to go into the next room and have a good
sleep; you had none last night. I'm going
to have a lay down, too, in a few minutes."

I lay down and slept as I had seldom slept in my
life. Next morning early we borrowed a saddle-
horse from Waller, and saying good-bye to the
kind people at the ranche, we "struck the trail,"
as they say in North America, and continued our
journey to Mr. Dunbar's ranche, which we
reached about six o'clock on the following evening.

What a glorious morning it was to be sure!
and how beautiful and fresh was wild nature in
that lonely wilderness—a wilderness in which
the prairie, the creek bottoms and the hill-sides

were carpeted with pink and clustering roses, lilies, and nodding sun-flowers that seemed to wink in the gentle breeze as with eyes of fire, blue larkspurs, blue-bells, purple and yellow violets, and a hundred other sweet familiar flowers. They say, truly enough, that on the prairie there is a flower for every day in the year. The prairie chickens, which were simply a splendid sample of grouse, strutted about in the bright sunshine on the hill-side, and several times on a grassy ridge, round which the almost imperceptible trail wound, or appearing on the brow of a valley, we startled a large band of graceful antelope, which stood to gaze for a minute or two and then bounded off at headlong speed. Now and again we passed solitary bands of cattle and horses, but as the country grew wilder and wilder, the valleys deeper, the table-lands higher, and the pine forests denser, we left behind all traces of any civilization. It was a veritable No Man's Land, a country in which nobody lived.

Acting on the rancher's advice I had brought a fishing line along with me, and when at noon we stopped for dinner at a deep, still lake, the rocky sides of which were shrouded by sweet, aromatic, odorous pines, I improvised a fishing rod of wolf-willow, and cast my line. In a few minutes I had landed three or four beautiful lake trout, which very soon were frizzling on a wood fire alongside our camp kettle. How delicious were those trout, how sweet the bread, how fragrant and refreshing the tea, and how picturesque our surroundings! We were, unless the red man was lurking somewhere in the neighbourhood, the sole occupants of' that glorious mountain land. One thing I became aware of in the North-West Territories was that the air was always dry and exhilarating, or, as I once heard a doctor say, highly charged with ozone, and the sun always shone down brightly from a cloudless sky. Mr. Dunbar was the very best of companions, and told me many fascinating stories of adventure pertaining to the early days. These I may tell some other time.

That night we picketed out our horses in a little grassy valley, alongside a running stream. We cut down slender pine boughs, covered them with a thick layer of dry grass, and rolling our blankets around us were soon in the land of dreams.

We were up by daylight next morning and off again, for it was Mr. Dunbar's intention to make the ranche that evening. Then through more wild country until at last we came out on the other side of the mountains, and began to descend a great bench that sloped towards the south. We were now on the Mississippi watershed. One thing that puzzled me on the open country was the immense quantity of bones and horns that were scattered about everywhere; indeed, entire skeletons of animals were frequently met with. I asked the rancher what these were.

"Something rather pathetic," he answered, "they are the bones of the innumerable vast herds of buffaloes that used to swarm all over the North American prairies. Of course, you've read Mayne Reid and Ballantyne and know all about them? They were, only a few years ago, so thick that I've seen the steamboats compelled to stop in the Mississippi until a herd had swum across. From a butte—that's a hill out here—I've seen the prairie simply black with them for miles and miles around me; there were millions upon millions!"

"But where have they all gone to now?" I asked in astonishment. "I certainly have read that they are rather scarce in these days, but it surely cannot be true that they have nearly all disappeared?"

"Quite true," he answered somewhat sadly, "they were killed for the sake of the skins. When the country was opened up, organised bands of hundreds of hunters literally shot them down by the thousand, and the carcasses—very good meat too, there was on them—were allowed to rot on the prairie; these dry bones speak for themselves. Sportsmen—save the mark!—from the Old Country also came out and assisted in the massacre, and went back to boast of how many hundreds of those truly noble and inoffensive creatures—the natural denizens of this great land—they had helped to wipe out."

"But would not they have had to go anyhow?"

I asked. "You could not have had cattle and horse ranches had they still lived."

"That's so," he replied, "we could not have kept our herds together had they remained in such vast numbers; but there is still room, and will be for many a long year to come, for thousands upon thousands of buffalo. If they had been allowed all the country north of the Canadian Pacific Railway, or say the Saskatchewan River, they would not have interfered with anyone. The great mistake was in not, to a certain extent, preventing them, and stopping the wholesale killing in time. However, there are a few small mobs still in this neighbourhood. I hope you'll have the good luck to see one, for five years from now and they'll be as extinct as the dodo, unless a few are caught and saved by private enterprise."

"And what about the deer, and the bears?" I asked. "As for the antelope I see there are still lots left."

"The deer are getting scarcer," he replied, "but in this particular country, which is still wild and uninhabited, it is, as you have seen, quite a common thing to come across a band of say from fifty to sixty antelope. As for the bears, they're on the increase; you see the half-breeds and Indians do not hunt them down as in the old days. They are a great nuisance to me, those great cinnamon bears, for they came down out of the woods, particularly in the spring, and kill my calves. We'll have a bear hunt one of these days."

About ten o'clock in the forenoon I saw a very wonderful sight indeed. We were still at a very considerable altitude and commanded a prospect of vast proportions, a world of rolling grey, save where a lake gleamed blue in the far distance in its setting of snow-white alkali-covered shores. The day was very hot, and as I looked southwards, towards what the rancher told me was American territory, I suddenly caught sight of something that hitherto had escaped my notice. It loomed up as if from the very edge of the horizon, and was a great city with walls and battlements, strange irregular buildings with towers and immense domes as in an Eastern city, only some of these domes were inverted in the most fantastic fashion and seemed top-heavy. I never in my life had seen or read of such a fantastic style of architecture. The tone of the whole was a dull grey.

"What city is that?" I cried in astonishment.

"It is no city, only a mirage," replied the rancher, smiling, "that city is the Bear-paw mountains in Montana. Those angular walls and buildings you see are the mountain sides distorted by some trick of unequal refraction, those curious inverted domes are simply part of the mountain tops seen upside down. Quite realistic, isn't it? However, it's no uncommon sight on these prairies."

In half an hour the weird scene had changed and vanished. About six o'clock in the evening we caught sight of the ranche buildings.

CHAPTER X.

A STRANGE JOURNEY.

THE buildings at Mr. Dunbar's ranche were not unlike Waller's, only there were more of them, and mostly as large again. They nestled snugly in a little meadow that cut into a hill-side, and as a creek described a half-circle round them and flowed within a hundred yards of the rancher's house, fringed with a wealth of cottonwood trees and wolf-willow, it was decidedly a pretty place. Mr. Dunbar said that as there was no room for me in the men's quarters I would have to be content with the dwelling-house. It is my belief that he merely said this as an excuse for keeping some one in the house whom he could talk to, for the only other occupant was old Ben, the cook, whose sole topic of conversation was the glory of the old days and the decadence of the new.

The cowboys, of whom there were several, were known by some of the most extraordinary nicknames I ever heard in my life. There were Broncho Pete, Bar H. Bill — referring to the cattle brand of some herd with which he had once been associated—Woolly Ned, Boko Jack, and others of a like incomprehensible character. These gentlemen ran to much back hair, leather overalls, strange forms of speech, and revolvers, after the manner of most cowboys, but otherwise they were a hard-working and steady lot. It is only the sham, shoddy article who preys like a parasite upon civilisation in the little frontier towns, and the cowboy of penny dreadfuls, who indulge in unaccountable and indiscriminate shooting and blackguardism. With them at first I was naturally an object of some curiosity, but as I went to the ranche dressed in a pair of mole-skin trousers, a broad-brimmed cowboy hat, and a checked shirt rolled up at the sleeves, my personal appearance at least escaped comment. When they found that I did not "put on side," and was anxious to make myself efficient in the usual duties connected with a cattle and horse ranche, they treated me very considerately indeed, although not infrequently betraying a disposition to practical jokes and romancing.

As I mostly went about with Colin Dunbar himself, and he seemed to take a pleasure in initiating me into the details of my work, I soon grew to like it. The healthy out-of-door life, as the rancher himself said, was making a man of me, and I never felt fitter in my life. I had written to Muriel Wray, telling her all about my adventure with the Indians, and concerning the ranche, and I did not forget to tell her how much I owed to my friend and employer, Colin Dunbar,

I had always hated letter-writing, but somehow I enjoyed writing that letter to her; the remarkable feature of the case was that it should be to a girl. On an average we managed to get a mail about once a fortnight; it was wonderful how interested I became in its probable arrival.

On one occasion we were visited by a Mounted Police patrol, which had some strange news to communicate. In the days of which I write it must be borne in mind that the Prohibition Law was in force — that is to say, no spirituous liquors, not even beer, were by law allowed to be sold in the North-West Territories of Canada without special permit. This law was made in the first place in the interest of the half-breeds and Indians, who become speedily demoralised when they have access to the fire-water of the Pale-face. But when the whites began to settle in the country they rebelled against the law, and the result was that the forbidden drink was smuggled into the country in greater quantities than if it had been allowed to come in under reasonable restrictions. Bringing the liquor in from the United States, and running the gauntlet of the Mounted Police patrols was one of the favourite methods of the smugglers; and despite captures, confiscation of property, heavy fines, and even long terms of imprisonment, they had of late been operating on a larger scale than ever. But the country through which these smugglers travelled was of such vast extent that when the police with their Indian and half-breed scouts did manage to drop across them, it was little better than chance work. Of late it had been discovered, that somewhere in the neighbourhood of Mr. Dunbar's ranche there was some means by which the smugglers managed to bring in their goods without as much as leaving signs of their presence behind them in the form of tracks. It was indeed a mystery that defied all clearing up, for not even the rancher or any of his cowboys ever came across the smugglers, or any signs of their having passed through the neighbourhood. One of the strangest features of the case was that those engaged in the illicit traffic did not look upon it as either criminal or sinful; they blamed the law instead. The police stopped a couple of days on the ranche and then went on towards the Milk River Ridge.

It was now October, and the Indian summer lingered still in the pine-clad valleys, on the breezy heaven-girt plateaus, and the brown, sun-dried prairies where the dim horizon line and sky become one. We had been over to Waller's to assist him in his big annual round-up, and he with his men had come over to assist us in our's, and a busy time of it we were having. As our cattle roamed over a tract of country several hundred square miles in extent, of course it meant a few weeks' work; for at various points they had all to be gathered into bands, and the calves and such young animals as had escaped previous round-ups, lassoed, thrown and branded. We had been shifting camp every day for about a fortnight, on the prairie and in the valleys that ran far into the mountains. Our spell of hard work was nearly over, and we had branded an unusually large number of calves. It was Sunday, and we were at the extreme western limit, if not beyond it, of Mr. Dunbar's country, and wild country it was, with its "bad lands," upon which nothing grew, yawning canyons piercing the mountain-sides, belts of thick pine forests and network of deep, still lakes.

Sunday morning on the prairie, and a well-earned day of rest, for Colin Dunbar, wisely, would allow no work to be done on that day but what was really necessary. We were camped in a beautiful valley, close to a shady grove of cotton-wood trees; the men had finished breakfast, and were scattered about engaged in certain little domestic duties peculiar to bachelors who have no womankind to mend their clothes or sew on buttons; the horses were picketed hard by; the cook was overhauling his spacious wagon to find the ingredients for the ever-welcome and invariable Sunday's duff, and the rancher and myself were sitting on the grass outside our tent talking about the difference between a Sunday morning in dear old England and a Sunday morning in that primeval wilderness. I had been up early washing my spare clothes, and so was practically free for the day Somehow that far-stretching canyon, which pro sented a wall-like barrier to our further progress west, fascinated me; what sounded like a fairy-tale concerning some long inaccessible lake that lay on the other side of it roused in me afresh all the old spirit of romance and adventure in my nature. I longed to look upon those mysterious and silent waters which even the red man shunned, as certain islands in it were looked upon as the haunts of lost spirits, the place where all bad Indians were condemned by the Great Spirit to wander after death. I asked the rancher if he thought it possible for me to get there and back before evening; I could take some bread and meat with me by way of dinner. He hesitated for a minute before speaking, then said—

"I've only seen the Lake of the Lost Spirits once, and then it was only by accident that I dropped across it. You see, the existence of the lake is generally accepted as a myth because it is practically inaccessible, and only one or two white men have ever seen it. The Indians regard it with superstitious dread, and can hardly be got to acknowledge its existence. There is no such thing as approaching it on horseback. It is hemmed in by precipitous cliffs, and no one knows whether it has an outlet or not. I saw it three years ago, when I set out to look for it from this very camp. It is actually not more than three miles from where we are now. There is only one place in the face of that high cut bank by which you can get to the top, but I can't let you go alone. I myself have to ride back to the ranche to-day."

"Then, sir, I'll get some one to go with me," I replied. "There's Broncho Pete; he's never seen the place, and is dying with curiosity to prove that it really exists. I know he has grave doubts about it. We had a long talk regarding it yesterday, and he told me how he had tried several times to find a passage over these mountains, but had always failed. With your permission I'll go and ask him."

The rancher gave his consent, and I went over to where Broncho Pete was engaged in spreading out a shirt, which he had just washed, on a raspberry bush. He was a typical cowboy in appearance, with this difference, that he was of a much more intelligent and inquiring turn of mind than the generality of cowboys. He had lived all his life on the prairies, and like most thoughtful men who have been much alone with wild Nature, and have carried their lives in their hands from day to day, there was a certain rugged dignity and air of self-respect about the man, because he recognised a higher power than himself. He was one of the cheeriest souls one could possibly meet, and although he was forty years of age, he had the fresh spirits of a boy. We had struck up a friendship shortly after I had arrived on the ranche, and in return for the many things I had to tell him about England, and what I had learned at school, he gave me many valuable hints in regard to my duties. He was one of the most successful "broncho busters" (*i.e.* horse-breakers) in Assiniboia, which accounted for his odd cognomen. He had a strong love of the wonderful in Nature; the spirit of adventure also ran hot in his blood. When I got over his brigand-like appearance, his fierce mustachios, his long hair, and expressive, if idiomatic, form of speech—simplified in this story—I found him a capital fellow.

Would he go with me to the Lake of the Lost Spirits if Mr. Dunbar showed us the way? Of course he would, and in less than two minutes he had divested himself of his great jangling spurs, and leather chaperagos—why he should have had them on just then is one of those things that only cowboys can explain—and we were talking softly to the cook in order to secure as good a lunch as possible for the occasion.

Mr. Dunbar led us up the valley for about a quarter of a mile, then ascended the thickly wooded hill-side until he reached the great precipitous cliffs of clay, which, like a mighty wall, ran north and south far as the eye could reach. It was honey-combed and tunnelled in a most fantastic fashion. Gigantic pillars of clay stood in front of the caves, reminding one of the fluted columns that guard the portals of tombs in Eastern lands. The cliff was at least two hundred feet high. How was it possible to scale it? But the rancher followed it along for a few hundred yards due north, then stopping at the mouth of a cave, the floor of which shelved

H

upwards in a most peculiar fashion, he remarked
with no little animation :—

"Here it is ; I was just a little afraid I might
not recognise it again ; one cave is so like
another. But this one is merely a sort of water-
course, as you see ; the water in the country
above has gradually worn its way through
fissures and the soft clay until it has struck this
cave and you can guess with what results. If
you follow it up, you will reach daylight and the
Land Mysterious in several minutes. Whatever
you do, for goodness sake don't lose your way,
or perhaps you'll not be able to get out of it
again in a hurry. I see, Pete, that you've got a
tomahawk ; a wise precaution, for you can blaze
your way."

He gave us certain directions how to reach
the lake. We then thanked him for his goodness in taking us so far, and he went back to the
camp.

Then we turned inwards to the cave. We
walked up its shelving, water-worn floor for
some twenty yards or so, then found that, doubtless since the rancher's visit, a huge boulder of
clay had become detached from the roof and
effectually blocked our way. But we discovered
a hole, hardly of greater width than our bodies,
through which the water had forced a passage,
and crawled through to the other side, where we
found ourselves in utter darkness. Lighting a
candle, which we had brought with us, we again
continued our strange journey. It gave one a

curious, eerie sensation to be thus, as it were, groping our way into the bowels of the earth. The passage turned and twisted about in a most bewildering fashion, but always led upwards. At one place we had to skirt a deep pool of water; at another we had to dig steps in what looked like the face of a miniature water-fall, and then we passed into a long gallery where there was a semi-twilight. Immediately our candle was blown out, and the air was filled with a most unearthly shrieking and flapping of wings; for the moment I was inclined to think that we had found our way into the underground haunt of the lost spirits. Broncho Pete gripped me by the arm.

"Stidy thar!" he remarked, in his usual easy and nonchalant way. "It's only the bats; we shan't be long before we strike daylight again, and to tell you the truth I won't be sorry. There's summat very uncanny about critters that won't face the light o' day."

I quite agreed with him as we passed out of the long passage amid the deafening turmoil our unexpected entrance had created. Turning a sharp bend, we came to a spherical chamber which tapered towards the outlet at the top, reminding one of the neck of a bottle, and knew that we had passed through the face of the cliff, and were once more in touch with the outer world. A fallen tree and some drift-wood lay across the mouth of the opening. Pete cleverly lassoed a short, projecting limb, several feet above his head, with a short, supple rope of greenhide he had taken the precaution to bring with him, and swarmed up it hand over hand. He managed with some difficulty to get astride of the fallen tree, and then I also followed his example. I had no difficulty whatever in doing this; few public school boys would have had any. We scrambled off the tree on to the bank, and found ourselves at the bottom of a deep, dry pool in a darkened pine-clad ravine. We were now in the Indian's dread Land of the Lost Spirits.

CHAPTER XI.

IN THE LAND OF THE LOST SPIRITS.

It was as if we had found our way into another world and that a weird one, for when we had scrambled out of the deep, brackened-lined, pine-shrouded ravine the trees and plants, and even the formation of the country, were quite different from anything we had ever seen before. There were giant trees of spruce and pine everywhere, and a medley of strangely fashioned boulders piled one atop of the other in the most fantastic manner possible. We ascended a long narrow ridge that the rancher had told us to look out for, and had a good look around before starting on our journey west. There to the east, in the direction in which we had come, was the brink of the great precipice, with here and there a gaunt, scraggy pine, either dying or dead, leaning in a sickeningly perilous fashion over the nightmarish depths below. It gave one a creepy sensation to look at them, just as one would get the cold shivers to watch a fool-hardy child get out of a dormer window and run along

8

the parapet of some dizzy wall in order to scare its nurse. Beyond that ledge, swimming in a bluish haze, we could see the distant prairie rolling away in a series of wave-like heights and hollows to a point where the earth and the sky became one. And all around us on this elevated tableland was a scene of savage, primeval grandeur—the sort of place that might have been from the beginning, before the evolving influences of the ages smoothed and toned down its ruggedness and its crudities.

"Say, Mister," suddenly remarked Broncho Pete, after an interval of silence, "I guess now you hain't got much to touch thet sort of thing in your country. Reckon you hain't got the elbow-room from what I kin larn. Is that so?"

"It's a different sort of scenery," I replied, unwilling to concede too much, "but there's one thing that I think you want really in your land-scapes, and that's variety in your skies—they're always the same day after day: nothing but a blank, monotonous pale-blue. You should see ours; we've got variety, I can tell you—an assortment of clouds, Pete, that would make you turn green with envy." One of Pete's amiable weaknesses was a desire to impress me with the superiority of all things American.

"Borack!" retorted Pete, with a show of contempt "Clouds—who takes stock in ugly, black clouds thet're always coming and going? What good are they I'd like to know?"

"They mean rain, anyhow, Pete," I remarked,

"and that's what you stand badly in need of on these same prairies."

"G'rlong wid ye!" exclaimed the cowboy, laughingly, as we both turned and began our journey westwards.

In some places the ridge we walked on was so broad that two or three coaches could have driven along it abreast. At other places it became so narrow that it put me in mind of walking upon the top of a wall. Then it would break off altogether, and it was only with the greatest difficulty that we could pick it up again, for off that ledge the ground was covered with such a chaos of rocks, and such a tangle of fallen trees and undergrowth that travelling was rendered impossible. Even the course of that erratic ledge was literally one of ups and downs. At times it rose up in front of us like the wall of a house, and again it shot suddenly down into a hollow. It was no wonder that the rancher had expressed his doubts as to whether we would be able to reach the lake. How he had been able to negotiate it alone, spoke volumes for his pluck. At one place, just on the brink of a deep hollow, we had rather an odd adventure.

Pete, who was unaccustomed to walking, was limping on ahead valiantly—he would have died rather than give precedence to me—when suddenly he turned, signing to me to crouch and approach with caution. Wonderingly I did so, and reached the rock behind which he had ensconced himself.

" Look thar," he observed, with a look of animation in his dark eyes, pointing to something in the hollow. " Isn't it a purty sight ? "

I looked, and I confess the " purtiness " of the sight made my heart leap into my mouth, and made me for the moment wish that I was anywhere but in that neighbourhood. Climbing the opposite side of the hollow was an immense cinnamon bear, a bear which is so large and fierce that it is often confounded with the grizzly— with two cubs following close at its heels. I knew only too well that a she-bear with its young was one of the most dangerous animals to meet under the sun. We would not have the ghost of a chance to escape from her rage if once she smelt or sighted us. I wondered what Broncho Pete seemed to find amusing in the situation. He took up a stone about the size of a cricket ball and poised it for a moment in his hand. What on earth did he intend doing ? Was the man mad that he was thus going to reveal our presence to the fierce brute !

Before I could stop him he had hurled the stone fairly at the bear and struck her sharply on the hind-quarters. Then something happened which even now as I write makes me laugh, although I could not but think at the time that it was a mean trick to serve Mrs. Bruin and her young ones. In all probability this bear had never seen a human being in her life, so not taking any foreign intruder into her calculations, she naturally supposed that one of the cubs was forgetting itself and playing a little practical joke upon her all on its own account. It was an occasion for prompt reprisal. She turned quickly, and not knowing which of them was the probable culprit—they both looked so very innocent—she gave each of the surprised youngsters such a sounding smack on the side of the head with a brawny fore-paw that they were knocked head over heels and rolled to the bottom of the hollow. We promptly ducked at the same moment, but Pete seemed so tickled over the success of his little joke, that to my horror he fairly exploded with laughter, and rolled over on his back. I shook him in annoyance and dismay, and quite forgetting that my own voice was just as audible as his laughter, I cried:—

"Pete, I say, Pete, you silly ass, can't you keep quiet! If you don't we'll have the old bear on to us, and then we'll be in a jolly nice fix. I say—now then—get up for goodness sake, man—" And I shook him again in order to bring him to his senses.

"Fancied it was the young uns!" he gasped between his bursts of laughter. "Great Cæsar! if that bear ain't a caution, she——"

But he did not finish his sentence, for the old lady herself at that very moment poked her nose round the corner of the ledge, and stood within a few paces of us, the cubs bringing up the rear, but at a more respectful distance than they had hitherto observed. The change of expression on Pete's face was ludicrous in the extreme, still, even then, with the huge, fierce brute looking at us, and probably unconscious of the real state of affairs, I could not help laughing. Pete sprang to his feet, seized the Winchester, and, facing the bear, cried :—

"Git up a tree, pardner, just as slippery as you like. I'll stand the ole lady off."

"Then you get up one, too," I rejoined, and turned to obey his orders with all possible despatch. But just at that moment Mrs. Bruin stood upright on her hind legs, and with great ungainly strides came towards us.

"Keep off, you old fool!" cried Pete, with a coolness for which I had hardly given him credit. "I don't want to use force to a lady, 'specially when she's got sich an interisting family, but—now then, not an inch farder, please!"

Nine men out of ten would have fired at the bear then and there, but under the circumstances Pete did not care to shoot. He understood bears by reason of a long experience with them. I was just preparing to climb a pine tree, when fearing that Pete was taking uncalled for risks by his tender-heartedness, I turned and caught up what once before had stood me in good stead, a stone somewhat larger than a cricket ball. I had read that a judicious poke in the ribs will double up the biggest bear that walks. With this stone I would double up Mrs. Bruin. It was an ungallant action, I admit, but there was nothing else for it. In another moment I had done it, and with a hoarse growl the bear fairly hugged herself with dismay and came down on her knees. I turned my attention to the tree and cried to Pete to make himself scarce also.

But a bear is one of the most knowing creatures under the sun, and it had no intention of letting me escape so easily. Before I had got three feet from the ground Mrs. Bruin had recovered herself, and made a dash at me. I swung my feet clear of her great claws just at the same moment as there was a flash and a roar, and she spun round swiftly, snapping at an unget-at-able part of her body. The bullet had only stung her up a little, and embedded itself harmlessly in a thick layer of fat. I looked at my companion as I swarmed up my particular pine, and saw with satisfaction that he was preparing to follow my example. But the bear turned her attention to Pete, and made a rush in upon him. With an agility that did the cowboy infinite credit he put the tree between himself and the bear, and watched her narrowly. There was no time to put the rifle to his shoulder and fire. Suddenly, and before the bear could divine his intentions, he had sprung into the air caught a branch over his head, and was pulling himself up. The bear arrived just in time to grip the stock of his rifle. She pulled it from his hand, and then favoured us with a little exhibition of a bear's strength when it is inclined to be nasty. Mrs. Bruin caught the barrel between her great jaws, and with one great, lever-like paw gripping the stock, and another gripping the muzzle, she snapped and doubled the rifle up as if it had been made of papier-maché. Pete's rifle was now, as he himself ruefully described it,—"an ilygint wreck."

"Bad luck to you!" he cried, looking down with disgust and chagrin depicted on his face, and addressing the bear, "if I'd suspected as how you couldn't take a joke, I'm blowed if I'd have played with you—thet's all!"

When Mrs. Bruin had crunched up the rifle into something unrecognisable, her feelings seemed relieved. She leisurely made for the foot of the tree which contained Pete, and gazed upon him with her small, cunning, dark eyes in a way that was irresistibly comical. She seemed to ask him which of the two had the best of the joke now.

Seeing that the broncho-buster's love of fun and recklessness had brought us into this fix, and that he did not seem to fully appreciate the gravity of the situation, I thought he wanted reminding of these things.

"Pete," I cried in a voice of concern.

"That's me," was the response. "What's up?"

"Nothing's up," I replied, "but something's down. I'm rather afraid I've let my handkerchief drop and that the bears may get it. Do you mind getting down, like a good fellow, for a minute and picking it up?" And I looked at him entreatingly.

Pete's face was a study. It was one at any time, seeing that his nose could hardly be called straight, and owing to a slight obliquity in his right eye which always made one uncertain as to whom he was addressing. As it was he gazed in my direction solemnly for a moment without speaking, and then with an odd twinkle in his whole eye remarked :—

"I guess, young man," said Pete, "you'll die young. You're too self-denying to live long. I really couldn't think of taking the lead in a case like this,"—he waved his hand with a deferential sweep in the direction of Mrs. Bruin—"after you please."

But I was quite comfortable in that pine.

As for the cubs, they came to the foot of my tree and went through quite a nice little acrobatic performance as if for my special benefit. Queer little creatures they were, looking for all the world like animated balls of fur. They gambolled and rolled over each other like puppy dogs amusing themselves, every now and again pausing to look up at me with sly side-glances. I verily believe they wanted me to come down and play with them. To tell the truth, I would have liked nothing better, but I was afraid that their mother might object to their playing with other children, so stayed where I was. When I looked at them and then at the broken gun, I thought it was a great pity that bears ever grew up at all. However, Mrs. Bruin evidently did not care about wasting her time at the foot of trees which she could not climb, so a few minutes later she trotted off in a southerly direction trying to look as if she had an appointment to keep, the cubs reluctantly following her.

"S'long!" yelled Broncho Pete after their retreating forms, and kissing his hand. "Sorry you couldn't stop to dinner. Guess your old man don't git fooling round you much."

We got down from our trees.

"Pete," I ventured, let's bar bears next time"

"You bet, boss," he remarked sadly, with a wan smile playing upon his thoughtful countenance.

We were now utterly without firearms; the only weapons we had were the knives in our belts. As the bears had evidently gone for good, there was nothing to fear on their account, but strangely enough, as we pursued our way eastward, my fancy converted more than one blackened rock and tree stump into something that looked very like a bear.

At last we lost the friendly ridge altogether and continued our journey over some of the roughest country I ever had the ill luck to tackle. We clambered over rocks and forced our way through thorny undergrowth until our clothes were only fit for the rag-man. At last when we had begun to think that somehow we must have gone astray, we came to an untimbered ridge running north and south; ascending it we came upon one of the most remarkable scenes it was ever my lot to witness. It was the Lake of the Lost Spirits!

We stood on the brink of a mighty, encompassing cliff, that fell sheer away without a break for four hundred feet and more, and at the foot of it lay the still waters gleaming coldly in the sunlight like a great band of burnished silver. With a lordly, crescent-shaped sweep it stretched out and on to the far south-west, until a great, dun-coloured precipice, streaked fantastically here and there with dull, furtive reds, and glaring yellows, cut it off from our sight. Away to the north it opened out and assumed the form of a bay thickly studded with wooded islands. But always hemming it in there were those stern, inviolable cliffs crested with giant sombre pines. But perhaps the most uncanny feature of this weird, isolated scene, was the utter stillness that prevailed ; it was a silence which suggested that of the grave. There was no song of bird, or sound of rill in that wild spot—it might have been a landscape in some dead planet whirling in illimitable space.

"No wonder the Injuns won't come within miles of this place," remarked Broncho Pete, after a pause. "Hark! what was that ? I'm blessed if it didn't sound like a gun !"

"Nonsense!" I exclaimed, "there's not a living soul nearer than the camp, and that's four miles off at least."

But for all that I had heard something, but ascribed it to some loose rock falling from the cliff into the lake.

We followed the edge of the cliff round to the

north for over a mile, and came to a place where it was possible, with care, to descend to the beach below.   We had halted, and were scrutinising the steep, broken slope, when Broncho Pete suddenly seized me by the arm, and, pointing to a little cove far below, whispered :

"Do you see anything down thar?"

I looked keenly for a minute or two before replying.

"Yes, I do," I said, "I believe I see a boat!"

CHAPTER XII.

A MYSTERY REVEALED.

A BOAT! How could there possibly be a boat
on the Lake of the Lost Spirits, a place practically inaccessible to the outside world; hidden
away in one of the wildest spots in the Great
Lone Land, the very existence of which, indeed,
was doubted by many? Had there been any
white men in that part of the country for any
length of time, the rancher or the police would
surely have heard of them.

But a boat it was, and that a goodly sized one,
we could even see the oars lying across the seats
from where we were. It was only by the merest
chance that we had caught sight of it, for being
moored behind a projecting rock it could not be
seen from any other point. Our astonishment on
seeing such a proof of occupation in that desolate
spot was just as great as if we had suddenly
come upon a party of Cockney picnickers
among the rocks. For a minute we were too
much surprised and lost in fruitless speculation
to speak. Pete was the first to break the silence.
He deliberately took off his broad-brimmed hat,

I

ran his fingers through his long hair, and ejaculated,

"Christopher Columbus!"

"Hardly," I said, recovering somewhat, "he's been dead too long; besides, he didn't come any farther than the sea-coast."

"G'long wid ye, poking borack at a chap like that!" retorted Pete, with a bright light in his business eye. "But who on earth can it be?"

"Let's go down and see," I replied. "There must be some one in the neighbourhood. Look, there is a sort of terrace that runs right down to it."

But Pete did not seem in any hurry. He had lived too long in the Wild West to be precipitate. He seemed studying every point of the compass. Suddenly he exclaimed,

"It may have bin fancy, and it may not, but I could have sworn as how I saw smoke rising from one of them islands a minute or two ago. Can't be anything very desperate anyhow. Yes, I guess we'll go and investigate," said Pete.

We had to exercise considerable caution descending the so-called shelving terrace, for at times it was so steep that the slightest slip would have precipitated us into the yawning depths below. At last we stood on the rocks alongside the boat, the painter of which was simply slipped over a narrow, upright piece of rock.

"They've gone ashore," observed Pete. "I fancy I warn't quite so far out after all, when I spoke about hearing a shot. As it's not likely that they'll be back for some little time, I've a notion for jest hevin' a look at them thar eye-lands. What d'ye think, mister?"

"I'm with you, Pete, it's a white man's boat anyhow, so we can't go very far wrong. Besides the first of the islands aren't more than three quarters of a mile away, and it would be interesting to find out where that smoke came from. Can you row, Pete?"

"Waal, don't know for I never tried, as the cove said when he was asked if he could play the fiddle."

"Then, I guess, I'll take the oars, which by the way are home-made, like the boat; there's no time to lose catching crabs."

"Time enough to say that, young man, when I begin to fish," rejoined Pete, to whom aquatic terms were evidently unfamiliar. "But jump in and let's start."

The oars were rather heavy, but I had always been fond of rowing, and on that still, calm surface it was not difficult to make head-way. Soon we were in among the islands in the middle of the lake, which must have been here at least a couple of miles in breadth. There was a regular group of them, some rising sheer out of the water to a considerable height, and nearly all covered with timber. It was one of the grandest and most picturesque sights I had ever witnessed, to look around upon that vast sea-cliff plumed with stately pine, surrounding us as with a mighty girdle. The water was so clear and calm that looking down we knew our eyesight was piercing many fathoms of water, but still we could not see the bottom. It was as if the crater of a great irregular volcano had been partially filled with water: that through the ages its lip and islands had been gradually timbered, and we were looking up towards its mouth.

We threaded our way among the islands and noticed that the sides of many were honeycombed in an extraordinary fashion, while some of them were of quite a respectable size. There was one right in the centre of the group, which rose to a considerable height above the level of the water. It must have been four or five acres in extent and was well-wooded, while its sides rose sheer up from the water's edge.

"Let's land here," I remarked, "and eat our lunch. There's a big cave over there which I think would be worth while exploring. Hilloa! I can see some planks and boxes in it. Some hunting party must have found out this place and established a camp here."

"But the boat?" observed Pete in a puzzled fashion; "that's what gits over me. I say, pardner, I'm blowed if I quite likes the look of things."

"Nonsense!" said I, and shot the boat right into the cave, on the other side of which there was a narrow ledge containing the signs of occupancy I had observed. We passed through what we had considered the mouth of the cave, and found that it was nothing more than a natural archway.

In a few minutes we were in a tiny bay with steep gravelly shores. To our astonishment we found a small landing-stage and a number of empty cases lying about. We made fast the boat and followed a small footpath that led up into a thicket of pine. Then all unexpectedly we came upon a small, circular hollow, and in the centre of it a collection of log-huts with sod roofs. From the rude chimney of one smoke was issuing. I caught myself rubbing my eyes in astonishment, for to find such signs of human habitation in a place that was supposed to be the headquarters of the Indian's ghost-world was something for which no one could expect to be prepared. Pete gripped me by the arm.

"Let's go back," he said. "I don't quite like the look of things! 'Pears to me thar's summat fishy 'bout all this. If I had only my shootin'-stick, now, it might be different."

But I pointed out to him that there was evidently no one on the premises; the owners were, doubtless, on the mainland, seeing we had their boat there could be no harm in having a peep into that shed since we were here.

Somewhat reluctantly Pete consented, and we walked over towards the building in question. It was of such ample proportions, and so peculiarly black and grimy, that instinctively I divined it was used for purposes other than human habitation. I looked at Pete, and he looked at me. There was an odd grin upon his face, and he winked his active-service eye. We entered by the low doorway, and the minute we did so I knew we stood in the bothy of whisky smugglers and illicit distillers! A large copper still stood on a raised stone platform in the middle of the room, and all around were bags of raw sugar, kegs of molasses, and others that evidently contained raw spirit. On shelves ranged round the walls were two-gallon stone jars, which we afterwards learned contained spirits that had been smuggled in from the States, while on the earthern floor various large tubs were scattered about in various stages of use, indicating, as Pete hurriedly whispered, that preparations were being made for an early brew. Indeed, in a small furnace a fire had evidently been only recently lit. In short, all the necessary requisites and appurtenances of the distiller's trade was here gathered before our eyes.

We realised that we had solved the mystery that had baffled the authorities and the Mounted Police so long—the main source from which the constant supply of smuggled and illicit spirits came that flooded that part of the province. Here was the smugglers' headquarters, but where were the smugglers ? We rightly guessed that if they had all gone ashore it was only for a very short time, for on the bench lay one or two articles of wearing apparel as if they had just been recently cast off.

"Pete," I exclaimed, "it's easy enough now to understand what the police inspector said to Mr. Dunbar about the smuggling mystery. This is the half-way house and hiding place of the smugglers between the United States and the belt of civilisation alongside the Canadian Pacific Railway line."

"Thet's so," observed Pete, "and that boat must take the goods from one end of the lake to the other where you can bet they've got some secret passages in and out of their own. But I guess the sooner we get out of this the better. If any of them should happen to catch us here they'll pot us as sure as little apples."

"What! Shoot us?" I exclaimed in some surprise. "What would they want to do that for?"

"Waal, you air jest green," was the cool explanation. "Do you suppose for one single second thet these 'ere crooks er going to show us perlitely back to the camp so's to let us blow the gaff on them—waal, you do take the cake! Come on; let's clear."

"*Just one moment, please. But first put up your hands or we'll blow you both into little bits before you can say Jack Robinson!*"

We wheeled round in consternation on hearing these words, which were uttered in a hard, dry voice. And there, standing in the doorway, were three men, each of them looking at us from behind a rifle or revolver!

CHAPTER XIII.

A GRIM ALTERNATIVE.

I HAD often read about people being told to "put up their hands" in stories of adventure, without quite understanding why it was necessary to perform such a seemingly idiotic action, but now it flashed across my mind that it was to prevent the hands straying to one's hip-pockets or revolver pouches if such playful little toys were carried. But as it happened we had neither, and even if we had possessed any it would have been the height of folly, and would probably have meant death to let our thoughts stray to them under the circumstances.

The three men who stood in the doorway with their respective weapons levelled straight at our heads were desperate-looking customers. They were all in their shirt-sleeves, and two of them were bare-headed. They were not unlike cow-boys, only there was a determined and wide-awake look about them that hinted at the dangerous nature of their calling. The third man who had acted as spokesman to the party, and was evidently the leader of the gang, filled me at once with wonder and aversion. He was tall, clean-shaven, pale, and put me for all the world in mind of a priest. His cold, grey eyes were inscrutable, but there was determination, and something very like asceticism in the indrawing of his hollow cheeks and the firm set of his thin lips. He wore his pale-brown hair rather short, and there was a hint of intellect and cold-bloodedness about him that plainly denoted he was not to be trifled with. To look into his keen, calm eyes was to recognise a master spirit.

With something like an exclamation of disgust Broncho Pete raised his hands above his head. But still he took the whole affair so coolly and so much as a matter of course, that I concluded it was not the first time he had been by force of circumstances compelled to perform the same feat. I was more surprised in another minute on discovering that the tall, ascetic leader of the gang had been recognised by my companion.

"Campbell," said Broncho Pete, "guess as how you've got the drop on me this time. Now that you hev got it, what's your little game?"

"Before I can answer that we'll have to tot up old scores. I don't forget that you were on the Vigilant Committee that time on the diggings in Dead-horse Gulch when I and a few more of the boys had to quit in the dead of winter and just when we were making a tidy little pile. Yes, I think I owe you something for that, Broncho!" and the ascetic one smiled in an evil fashion.

"Yes, thet's so; I remember," coolly rejoined Pete. "You were as crooked a lot of pur-fessional rooks as ever used marked cards or loaded dice. I don't mean to say that some o' them who played with you weren't quite as bad as yerselves an' didn't deserve to be took in, but you were a tough crowd, and if you kin rekelect, it was lucky for you they didn't lynch you over that Simons racket. If it hadn't been for me you'd have got strung up, and you owe me something for thet, Mr. Man!"

"I never forget anything, but at the same time who the dickens invited you into this ranche? And just be good enough to tell your young friend to put up those hands of his above his head, until he's been searched, or we'll feed the fishes in the lake with him."

"You're just what I thought you were—a great, big bully!" I burst out, no longer able to contain myself on hearing this fresh avowal of the fellow's cold-bloodedness. "You might see we've got no firearms, and a jolly good job for you we haven't. If we had you'd not look quite so cock-sure of the situation. You're a cowardly brute, that's what you are!"

For a moment an ugly glitter came into the long one's eyes, but he only smiled and in that quiet, passionless voice of his observed—

"You'd better keep a civil tongue in your head, youngster, or I'll have you birched. Turn out your pockets and look sharp about it!"

There was something so mocking and humili-ating in the command that I fairly lost my head. Clenching my fists, I squared up to him.

"You just try and birch me," I gasped. "If it weren't for that pistol you hold in your hand you'd be afraid to say as much. You just try and touch me!"

"Jim," said Campbell, turning to one of his followers, "keep Broncho Pete covered with your shooting-iron and blow his blooming head off if he moves a finger. Bill, you give me your revolver and secure that cub. Tie his hands behind his back with that piece of rope you see in the corner."

Quicker than it takes to write it, the man called Bill had handed over his revolver to his chief, picked up the rope, and prepared to seize me. There was that look in his eyes which I once saw in those of a man who with halter in hand was preparing to strangle a dog.

"Now, Wally, old stocking,"—this was the nearest approach to a term of endearment that I ever heard Broncho Pete use—"jist keep your hair on, and don't git cutting up rough. It's no use; they've got the drop on us and no mis-take."

"Now thin, you young whipper-snapper, just give us your paws, will yer?" And the gentle-man named Bill caught me by the nape of the neck and twisted me round before I could quite make up my mind as to whether he really meant to use force or not.

I admit I did wrong in losing my temper. Had I only remained quiet it is unlikely that they would have attempted any further violence. As it was, Bill's sharp, humiliating action fairly took me by surprise, but with a sudden wrench I freed myself and struck out with both fists. As I stood on the defensive, expecting him to seize me, he suddenly raised his hand with the rope in it, and bringing it down sharply I realised that I was lassoed, the noose settled down over my shoulders. There was a sharp, unexpected jerk, and my arms were pinioned firmly to my sides. Another jerk and I found myself lying face downwards on the earthen floor. A twist of the rope, and it was obvious to me that I was securely bound and utterly powerless. I was chafing with rage, but realised that I had brought it all upon myself. It was a lesson I was not likely to forget for many a long day.

"Now then," remarked the ascetic one, "lay him across that bench and give him twenty with the rope's end. Youngsters who don't give in quietly want to be taught how to."

Before I could wriggle clear of them, Bill and the other ruffian picked me up and placed me across the bench. I kicked out with my feet; in another minute they also were made fast. It was an awkward position to be in, so awkward, indeed, that someone had to hold my legs to keep me in position. Being face downwards it was impossible to see what preparations were being made for my punishment. It was not long before those preparations were made **plain** enough to me.

Swish! and the bitter end of the rope descended on my back with no slight force. The pain was terrible, and though my first impulse was to cry out, by a strong effort of will I kept silence.

" *One*," sang out Bill with unction.

Swish! Again the rope descended and this time it was as if the hemp were cutting into my flesh. It was more than I could bear, and something like a groan escaped from my lips.

" *Two*," cried Bill again.

I waited with dread cut number three, and thought it must surely knock all the life out of me. But there was an interruption and I realised that it was Broncho Pete who spoke.

"Campbell," he cried, "for God's sake stop! You hev got down low. I've known you do many a shady thing, but I'm blest if I thought you'd conderscend to revenge yourself on a youngster."

Again the rope descended, and it seemed to me as if I must faint with the pain. As it was I could only moan feebly.

" *Three*," cried the ghoulish Bill with a ring of satisfaction in his voice.

"Oh, you infernal coward!" gasped Pete, "why can't you flog me as is tough and can stand it?—And I suppose you call yourself men!"

"Shut up, Broncho," snapped Campbell, "or

I'll bore a hole in your thick skull! You kin lay off now, Bill!" he concluded. "I guess the young'un 'ill keep a civil tongue in his head for the future. Will you promise me to behave yourself in future, youngster, if I let you up?"

"Yes," I gasped, realising that another stroke or two from that rope's end and I would be as good as dead. Besides what was there to be gained by mere bravado?

They unbound me and I was once more upon my feet, but so great was the pain of the cuts they had given me, and the unnatural, cramped position I had occupied that it was as much as I could do to stand upright. Then we were both searched to make sure that nothing in the nature of a weapon was concealed about our persons. When the smugglers had satisfied themselves that we were practically inoffensive, they ceased to cover us with their revolvers and we were a a little more at our ease.

"Where on earth did you come from? and what the dickens brought you here?" drawled the ascetic one looking at Pete curiously and feeling his chin with his left hand. His right held a revolver.

"Guess I had as much right to come here as you," retorted Pete. "I needn't ask what brought you here—I say, Campbell, this is a pretty, tidy little 'stablishment, and you've managed to run it a good long time, too, without being nabbed."

"Yes, and I mean to run it for some time

longer in spite of you having dropped across us.
The round-up won't see you two jokers for a day
or two." There was a hard inscrutable smile on
the man's face as he spoke that made my blood
run cold.

"Oh!" exclaimed Pete, airily, "you're going
to give us free board and lodgings are you, and
then what after that?"

"You're fishing, but I may as well tell you—
as I daresay you've guessed—that it's not very
likely we're goin' to allow you to go back to
civilisation and spoil our game, and perhaps
bring the Mounted Police down about our
ears."

"I guessed as much," remarked Pete, "but
what er you going to do with us? You can't
keep us here for ever."

"I don't know that there's any particular
reason why we should keep you at all," retorted
Campbell significantly. His thin lips came
together, and his clean-shaven face seemed the
embodiment of vindictiveness and determination.

"You daren't do it, Campbell," said Pete,
apparently unconcerned. "You're not sich a
blanked fool as to put a halter round your own
neck, and those who are with you, on this side
the lines. You seem to forget that they know
at the cattle-camp where we were going when
we set out, and they'll search every hole and
corner of this yere neighbourhood until they find
out where we've got to. Then there's the

Mounted Police with their half-breed and Indian scouts; and don't suppose they're going to let us disappear until they've found out what's become of us. You daren't do it, Campbell! You're a bad 'un I know, but you're not egzactly a fool. Well," said Pete, "What now? Better row us ashore again, and I'll guarantee we'll not split."

"There's a proverb which says" grimly remarked Campbell, eying us closely all the time "that 'dead men tell no tales.'"

"Pshaw!" snorted Pete, "what're ye givin' us? You've got queer ideas of satisfaction. Do you think it 'ud be worth the facing of a brand-new wooden scaffold behind the Mounted Police Barracks at Regina, and a drop o' six feet."

For a second—only for a second—I thought a sudden flash of fear came into the desperado's eyes, and for the first time he lost his apparently indifferent manner.

"Shut up, you fool!—if you keep jawing me like that, Pete, I'll give you an ounce of lead right now," he cried, angrily.

He paused for a moment as if considering, then in a determined but somewhat calmer manner, said deliberately:

"Now, look here, you two jokers, we're wastin' precious time and time's valuable to us just at present; we've got to put through another brew in a few minutes, and must come to an understanding. You'll admit that when you came here it was on your own invitation.

You ran your own heads into the bees' nest. Of course, it's not likely we're going to be such fools as to row you ashore again—you stole that boat from my mates, by the way, and they'll have a bone to pick with you when they get here—you'd only blow the gaff upon us. Oh no, I'm not taking any man's word. You know what the Scriptures say : ' All men are liars.' "

He paused and smiled upon us as if he were merely imparting some humorous information to boon companions. His reference to the Scriptures, and his obvious callousness, made my blood run cold, despite my efforts to keep cool. He continued :—

" There's only one way out for you, and that's to join us. You won't be asked to do any of the risky night work on the prairie, running our supplies and commodities in and out—that's for us old hands—but you can have a jolly good time here if you want to. You can have all the booze you want in moderation, Broncho ; we live like fighting cocks, and the youngster here can have all the literature he wants from Fort Benton or the cars on the C.P.R. This island's eight acres in extent and is big enough to hold us all ; there's good shooting and fishing, and, besides, there's money in the business. Eighteen months at this game and I'll guarantee you fifteen hundred pounds apiece. I'm going to quit the game in that time myself and going down south. You'll not make that in ten years on the ranche, Broncho. As for you, young man," he looked at me with less of vindictiveness in his eyes, and spoke pleasantly enough, " I guess you've got to make your way in the world, and it's one chance in a thousand for you. To have fifteen hundred pounds at the end of eighteen months to go into civilisation with, and to start yourself in some good-going business, is not to be sneezed at. Come now, what do you say ? "

I confess, to my shame, that for the moment I actually entertained the smuggler's project. When I was very much younger it had actually been one of the dreams of my life to be a full-fledged pirate in the Spanish Main, but I had long since discarded such an ambition as impracticable. Here, now, was an ideal life, one full of romance and adventure, which would just suit my tastes, and, moreover, there was money attached to it which would aid me in— what of late had been taking definite shape within me—the desire to embark in some specific line of life which would ensure my worldly fortunes. How I would like to go back to the Cedars and prove to my uncle and aunt, and perhaps more than anyone else to Muriel Wray, that I was no weakling, but one who was able to more than hold his own in the battle of life. Somehow, I had been thinking a good deal about my girl friend of late, and wondering when I would be able to pay back that twenty pounds she had lent me. It had begun to weigh upon my spirits like a nightmare

One curious feature of the case was that although I had written to her she had not answered my letters. But again, how was I to herd and associate with such men as Bill and his mates? True, there would be Broncho Pete, and there would be many distractions, but would I not soon get tired of the life? And there was my honest friend Colin Dunbar; how could I whom he had befriended be the means of causing him any anxiety, and, perhaps, something weightier still by my unaccountable disappearance? And Muriel Wray, what would she think if she wrote to me and received no answer? Of course, the news would be sent home that in all probability my companion and I had fallen into the lake over the cliff, and been drowned, and what an amount of wanton pain I might inflict on those whom I considered my best friends on earth. And then there was the most important side of the question—the moral side. What would my friends think of me if they knew of the traffic I was engaged in, and what would I think of myself? Fool that I was to even entertain such an idea! Campbell could kill me if he chose, but I would have none of him or his dirty work. Though these thoughts may take a minute or two to read on paper they flashed through my mind in a very few seconds. Campbell tapped his foot impatiently on the ground.

"Now then, Pete," he concluded, "what do you think of it?"

"If I say 'no' for both us, what then?" asked the cowboy quietly.

"Well, I'm not quite sure," replied Campbell with that curious pursing of his lips again; "but you can hardly expect us to hamper ourselves with you. We've got the drop on you, and there's the lake," he concluded, significantly.

Then I saw for the first time in my life how under an eccentric manner and rough exterior the soul of true nobility can exist. Pete threw one arm over my shoulder, and with a flush on his rugged, sun-browned face exclaimed,—

"Let me speak for us both, Wally, my boy. I've lived longer in the world than you, and I know what I say is right."

"Campbell, a clear conscience and our honour is worth more to us than your money. We will have none of it! Shoot us down if you dare, but remember there is a God who will call you to account if man fails to do it."

CHAPTER XIV.

A MAD SMUGGLER.

I FULLY expected that Campbell would put his threat into execution then and there; he did not look like a man who wasted words. I confess that Broncho Pete's heroic stand was a revelation to me; he was such a grotesque, cheery mortal that I had hardly credited him with a serious side to his character. Even now as I looked at him his irregularity of feature, which to say the least of it was decidedly comical in effect, became dignified by reason of the high resolve that stirred within him. And I had almost taken it for granted that Pete would join the smugglers and illicit distillers! How small it made me feel for having entertained such an idea!

Campbell toyed with his pistol for a moment or two with a peculiarly apprehensive look in his eyes as if he had not quite made up his mind what to do. Ruffian as he was, I believe the cowboy's speech alone stayed his hand. I feel certain that but for the fear of that unseen power which would avenge, so cold-blooded and vindictive was the man that he would have shot us down with as little feeling as he would have shot a couple of dogs. But still he was one of those who having made a threat before the men who looked upon him as being a law unto himself, he did not quite see his way to draw back from the position he had taken up. I confess to having been at first terribly frightened, but somehow that fearless look upon the cowboy's face, and the feel of his hand upon my shoulder, gave me heart of courage.

It is difficult to know what the desperado would have done had not at that very moment a couple of rifle shots rang out in the far distance. Such a remarkable series of echoes followed close upon them that one could have imagined the island was being bombarded from every point of the compass. Campbell listened attentively.

"It's the boys," he remarked, turning to his rough-looking mates, "they've missed their boat and are signalling to us. Bill, you'd better take the boat across to them and pick them up. Tell them we've got visitors who took the loan of the dingy."

Bill disappeared and I breathed more freely. It seemed as if we were to have a respite. Campbell turned his attention to us again.

"On second thoughts," he said, "I'll not give the fishes in the lake a treat just yet. You may come to take a more sensible view of the situation after a bit."

"Don't go a cent upon that, Campbell," returned Broncho Pete, "we're not going to do it. If you choose to row us ashore, as I said before, we give you our word of honour we ain't going to say a word about you. You're sure to be took sooner or later!"

"Your word of honour!" sneered the smuggler, with a cynical grin, "I think it was that chap called Pilate, in the New Testament, who asked 'What is Truth?' wasn't it, youngster?"

I replied in the affirmative, surprised that such a man should be familiar with and quote from Scripture. He doubtless saw the look of surprise and speculation in my eyes, for he said—

"You think it queer, youngster, to find me familiar with the New Testament, do you? Now, do you remember what Æschylus said about Truth?"

I could not remember what the Greek dramatist had said, so shook my head.

"Or Menander, or Polybius?" he asked, still watching me curiously, with the ghost of a smile playing about the corners of his mouth.

It was such an odd thing to meet a desperado with the Greek authors on the tip of his tongue that I stared at him in astonishment, all sorts of wild speculations running through my head.

"Oh, well," he remarked unconcernedly, "I could see you'd been a public school-boy, but I'm afraid you haven't made the most of your opportunities. However, in these days a classical education doesn't count for much. When I tried to make a living by it I jolly-well starved—that was my first take-down. Then after some little time I turned my attention to making whisky and smuggling, and have done well ever since."

"I don't see that you've got much to congratulate yourself upon," I remarked, gaining courage. "Some day you'll be caught, and then I don't see where your success will come in."

He laughed as if he really enjoyed my remarks.

"Oh, come now," he rejoined, "that's rather rough, you know. But you're young and have got to find things out yet. I'm sorry you were such a fool as to stray into these parts, for I believe there's the makings of a good man in you. But you've done it and must abide by the consequences. You'll find—if you're sensible and make up your mind to disappoint the fishes in the lake—that there's precious little sentiment in this mercenary world. In the meantime my mates will be here in a matter of fifteen minutes or so, and then we'll hold a species of court-martial. I'm inclined for once to think that you two have some respect for what some people call their word of honour. Will both of you sit over there on that bench and promise not to make a move either one way or another whiie we do a little work? If you don't we've got an orthodox dungeon cell, such as you read about in story books, that we'll clap you into, and I guarantee you'll not care about it. Come now, make up your minds."

"We'll sit here, Wally," said Pete. " If that

there dungin cell be anything like themselves
it's precious black and uncomfortable, you kin
bet your boots."

The ascetic one grinned.

"You promise?" he asked sharply, again
tapping the ground impatiently with his right
foot.

We both promised. The bench was placed
close to the wall between the two doors, and we
sat down.

"Now, I warn you," said our captor-in-chief,
"if either of you lift a finger or make an attempt
to escape, you'll be dead men in two shakes of a
lamb's tail. You couldn't swim in that lake anyhow. The water in it is so deadly cold that
you'd go down like lead with cramp before going
four yards."

We fully realised the truth of what he said, so
made up our minds to make the best of the
situation. Then for the first time our captors
took their eyes off us and set to work. They
stoked up the fire afresh, emptied a lot of liquid
into a large copper still, adjusted a long, zigzag
tortuous pipe called a worm, messed about with
various tubs and kegs, and became fairly engrossed in the making of spirit. Despite our
determination to have nothing to do with the
illicit distillers or their business, it is not too
much to say that Pete and I watched the various
processes with the keenest interest. The place
was scrupulously clean, and everything was done
quickly, methodically, and evidently with a prac-

tical knowledge of what was required. A pleasant sweet smell as of malting barley pervaded the large room; the sunlight streamed in through the shutterless window and the open doorway; the shadows among the pines outside, with the gleam of blue water at the end of a narrow cutting that ran down to the lake, and which was arched with honeysuckle and wild roses running riot among the boughs, made up a very peaceful and pretty picture indeed. It was hard to realise that this was the head-quarters and hiding-place of a gang of godless, desperate men.

"Wally, old stocking," whispered my companion, "keep your pecker up! I guess as how it'll all come right. They're trying on a game of bluff. That Campbell's a devil and no mistake, but he's an edycated man, and he knows that s'posin' he did want to pot us he couldn't even trust his own men. Them curs would split on him one of them fine days as sure as fate. Hello! here's the boat come back!"

Half an hour elapsed before the boat appeared. In it were four white men and an Indian. They jumped ashore and came up the narrow path while Bill took the boat round to the little natural harbour among the rocks. They had evidently been on an expedition to replenish their larder, for slung on a pole which two of them bore upon their shoulders, was a splendid black-tail deer. Another carried several brace of prairie chickens. They came into the hollow and entered the building.

Instinctively I scrutinised them to see if there would be a grain of mercy thrown on the scales in our favour when our court-martial came off. Two of them were ordinary-looking men, of good physique and self-possessed, not different from the cowboy one may meet on the prairie at any time, only theirs was that look of keenness and resource that one may see in the faces of those who have been accustomed to carry their lives in their hands. The third white man made me more hopeful. He could not have been more than four-and-twenty years of age, and was upon the whole a rather good-looking fellow. When his bright, brown eyes rested upon me for the moment, it struck me that there was a mute greeting in them, and that he looked rather sorry to see us in such a position. But it was the Indian who took me by surprise. As soon as my eyes rested on his face, it seemed as if my blood ran cold. It was Make-Thunder, the red-skin who had shot at Colin Dunbar and myself in the valley on our way out to the ranche, and who had escaped so cleverly from the clutches of the Mounted Police. There was no mistaking him ; his was the high, aquiline nose, the hawk-like, proud glance, and the lithe, athletic figure. But surer sign of all, he recognised me.

"Ough, ough!" he exclaimed, grinning down upon me in a way that made me feel decidedly uncomfortable. It was as if one brown hand were already grasping me by the hair of the head, and the other with a long, sharp knife in it were making a fanciful circle preparatory to relieving me of my scalp.

"You two seem to have met before," remarked Campbell, whose sharp eyes missed nothing.

"Oh, yees by-gar, we bin meet way back yondaire," glibly explained the Indian to my no little astonishment. "He try keel me an' maybe so I try keel him."

"Hello!" exclaimed Campbell, who, with the others, now stood a few paces off watching us; "this is interesting. How he do it, Make-Thunder?"

"Ough! I was near forget now. Eeet was in Fish Creek Coullee an' I was look out black-tail deer to take to tepee when nudder man Dunbar and dis boy come up 'long trail. I shoot pony b'longing to dis boy, an' den nudder man he keel Crooked-legs, who took out pony b'longing to Enjun and take dem 'way. Dis boy I was see 'im peek up stone an' trow it at Crooked-legs firs' time. Nex' day Shermoganish-peleece, she was come out an' come down Coullee. But you bet my medicine she goot, I was lay low 'longa rock lak as wile cat. Den I come out on to de prairie all same as peleece scout, an' peleece she no know. But dees boy she see me an' make big pow-wow an' geet hees gun. I catch pony an' ride 'way. Eet was de bes' pony I evaire have, by-gar! Dis boy he chase me lak he chase buffalo an' one time he shoot but he mees, den I shoot an' I was mees. Den I clear out an' was come here, by-gar!"

Then for the first time I heard Campbell laugh. When at Harrow an unfortunate usher had been seized with the dread disease of his family, insanity, and I saw him being taken away in a cab. He caught sight of me as I passed the carriage window and waving his hand he laughed in a way that made my flesh creep. Something in Campbell's hard, soulless cackle sent my thoughts back to that incident and startled me with a suggestion of its similarity. The other men grinned and looked at me in a curious fashion as they listened to the Indian's account of my doings. The youngest of the new-comers, in whose face it seemed to me there lay most hope for our safety, alone watched me with a thoughtful expression in his eyes, as if he were exercised about something. I noted that he was called Alan by his mates.

"Well, young feller," remarked Campbell when he had relieved his feelings, "it seems you're a bit of a terror, but it's only what I would have expected from you. It's a deuce of a pity Make-Thunder didn't pot you that time he shot your horse, or that time when you tried to pot him and missed, and he returned the compliment. It would have saved you from much of the misery there's in this wicked world. So you're a protégé of Dunbar's, are you? Now, I've got an idea. I owe that chap Dunbar a grudge; he's too enterprising by half, and more than once he's been perilously close to our trail. He wants warning off. Do you know what the brigands do in Corsica and other lively places when they want the friends of captives to hurry up with a ransom?"

I did not reply, but only looked steadily into the passionless grey eyes. I did not know what he might do if I took them off him.

"Then I'll tell you," he continued; "they just slice off a part of the captive's ear or chop off a finger and send it through the post to his relatives with the intimation that delays are dangerous, and that generally makes them hurry up. Now, if we sent something of the sort with an intimation to the rancher to keep at a distance, unless he wanted your head on a salver like that girl—Herodias' daughter I think she was—who managed to bag the head of John the Baptist, I fancy Colin Dunbar would lay low and not trouble us."

Again he laughed, and for the first time I noticed that the others exchanged furtive and significant glances. Immediately the thought flashed across my mind that this man called Campbell, if not already mad, was fast becoming so, and that the fact was more than obvious to his companions. Pete gave me a sharp nudge with his elbow as if to enjoin silence. For a minute there was a painful stillness. It was Alan who first spoke, and he did so without looking at me, and as if the subject were a matter of indifference to him.

"That's all very well, boss," he said, "and wouldn't be a bad idea if it were practicable, but it ain't, and would simply mean Stony Mountain Penitentiary and Sing-Sing afterwards for every mother's son of us." No, I guess we haven't long to run in this show anyhow, for I learn that the Police are going to establish a new detachment at Pend Oreille, and if so, the game is up, and we may as well quit as long as we've got the chance. We'd be fools to risk our necks for the sake of two such jokers. No, I vote we keep them here as prisoners until such time as we make tracks across the lines again, and then we'll let them go decently. It will be so much in our favour if ever we should happen to get into trouble. Besides, we can take them about to keep an eye on them, and we can make them work for their grub. It will be two men's work instead of one, and it will be as good as a rest for the man who does the watching."

I looked up into his face gratefully; I had thought the man had the feelings of a human being from the first. But he would not look at me, and I thought I divined the reason. Two of the other men seemed to consider Alan's speech favourably. Campbell seemed to be pondering over the matter. Suddenly he said :—

"I'll tell you what, boys, we'll settle their fate with the dice. There's nothing like a little gamble now and again." Get some paper, Alan, and tell Bill to come here. A cross—for I know

some of you didn't go to college—will mean a
funeral in the course of the day, and a round
nought will mean that they'll have board and
lodgings for a few months in return for their
enforced services. Come on, boys, into the
mess-room and I'll be croupier. It doesn't
matter a tinker's curse to me what becomes of
them either one way or the other. Pete, would
you like a drink of whiskey? I'll say this for
you, Broncho, that you never were mean, and if
you weren't much of a boozer yourself, you were
always ready to stand drinks for all hands."

I do not believe that Pete really wanted that
drink, but possibly he thought it would be bad
policy to refuse, so took the glass which the
uncanny smuggler-in-chief handed him.

"Here's to you, Campbell," he said with a
coolness that only a man could have felt who
had little fear of death in his heart. "But I've
one favour to ask of you an' thet's thet you only
have one ballot; an' thet's for me. You remember that affair of Simons? You owe me something for thet. Now, it doesn't matter a red cent
what becomes of me; I've had my day an' the
fishes in the lake will find it out when they come
to feed on this 'ere tough old carcass, but here's
Wally, as is a right good sort as you kin take
my word on, and, Campbell, I don't believe you're
such a low down chap as to tetch him. Isn't thet
so?"

"We'll see," answered the strange mortal
addressed. "Jim, you keep an eye upon them

and your finger on the trigger. An ounce of lead to the first one who makes a move."

He left the building and the others followed him.

To me the next ten minutes seemed an eternity. The cowboy sat with his arm passed through mine, but neither of us spoke a word. Where were all my bright dreams for the future now? Was it not an odd fate for an English boy only fresh from a public school to have hanging over his head—an ounce of lead or imprisonment in a lonely island with a gang of desperadoes? But my life had not been a particularly happy one. My uncle, Gilbert Derringham, had at one time been kind to me, and there were some other boys at Harrow whom I liked immensely. The girl, Muriel Wray, was surely the one human being of whom I had the brightest memories; after her came the rancher, Colin Dunbar, and my present companion.

Just then Alan entered the room and handed two pieces of paper to Jim. I thought he whispered something in his ear and the latter nodded his head. I could hear the murmuring of voices come indistinctly from an adjoining room. Were they never going to decide upon our fate? The delay in itself was a living death.

Then Campbell the smuggler entered the room and stood in front of us.

CHAPTER XV.

A STRANGE PRISON.

"WELL, gentlemen, I've come to tell you that you've got some little time to put in yet in this miserable vale of tears," drawled the scholastic smuggler-chief, as if he hardly expected that the matter would interest us. "And I may as well tell you, by the way, that you just escaped the fishes by the skin of your teeth. The throws were even, so we let Make-Thunder chip in. We said we'd let him decide about you, and the noble savage said that unless we were prepared to torture you—crucifixion or fire, or something of that nature—he elected to bide his time, and operate upon you in a tonsorial way—scalping I fancy he meant—when opportunity offered in fair fight. There's no accounting for the tastes of some people—especially bad Indians."

He addressed us in such a communicative and friendly fashion that but for the cold-blooded import of his words one would have imagined he was the best friend we had. The others now returned to the still-room, and the strange being continued.

"Now," he said, "I want you clearly to understand your position here. I can't exactly say how long circumstances will oblige us to avail ourselves of your services, but one thing is certain, that until things get too hot you've got to keep us company. I've got some of the Greek authors by me, young 'un, which, if you behave yourself, I'll allow you to peruse in your leisure moments. I've got an idea you wasted your time at school and, anyhow, I don't think that schools are what they used to be in my time. You'll be allowed a good deal of liberty, and will live just the same as we do ourselves, but remember, an attempt at escape means instant death."—He turned to the others—"You hear, boys, an ounce of lead apiece if you find them up to any monkey tricks: a four-bushel bag with a big stone in it, row them a mile or two out into the Lake of the Lost Spirits, close to where the outlet pierces the mountain, and there'll be no chance of them spoiling the water for domestic purposes. Jim, you keep an eye on them to-day until we make more definite arrangements. Now then, let's have dinner, for I feel rather peckish, Broncho, and Master—er—?"

"Derringham," I said.

"Well, Master Derringham, I'm sorry that we can't exactly invite you to dine at the same table as ourselves. It would be *infra dig*, you know, to have jailors and prisoners messing together—one's got to study the conventionalities more or less. Jim, you take them into the old

mess-room alongside Pierre's kitchen, and see
that they get plenty to eat. . . . And I say, Jim,
you *are* a dirty beggar and no mistake! Did
you wash your face this morning? Now, honour
bright, did you?"

"I don't see what it matters to you," was the
sulky reply. "What's the use of washin' every
day? I washed yesterday mornin'. You're
allus on the scrubbin' racket."

With something like a snort of contempt,
Campbell left the room.

It was as if a great load had been lifted from
my mind on discovering that we were not yet
doomed to take our departure from this life in
the very unsatisfactory manner that Campbell
had advocated. It was bad enough as it was to
think of all the trouble and anxiety we must
inevitably give to our friends when we did not
turn up again. The round-up would doubtless
apprize the Mounted Police of our mysterious
disappearance, and they with their Indian half-
breed scouts would make their way into the wild
Land of the Lost Spirits and scour the beach—
where there was any—at the foot of the great
cliffs for our bodies. There was little chance of
them discovering our presence on the island.
The buildings stood in a hollow with a thick
belt of timber effectually screening them, and
anyhow, if they did think of having a look at the
islands, which was extremely unlikely, without
a boat the task was impossible of accomplish-
ment. The smugglers would take very good

care to keep well out of sight for the next week or two. In all probability they only ran their cargoes of illicit goods during the night, and it was tolerably certain that for some little time they would not be so foolish as to light fires during the day which by their smoke would betray their presence. How Pete and I regretted that fatal spirit of enterprise and curiosity which had led us to take the boat in order to find out who lit the fire that sent up the smoke on the island! We had burned ourselves in that fire with a vengeance.

My reflections were interrupted by our jailor. He was a curious-looking customer, truly, and I was by no means surprised that a smart and seemingly fastidious man like Campbell had taken him to task on the score of cleanliness. He had a luxuriant head of hair and an immense beard, and what was seen of his face, neck, and chest was the colour of mahogany. The shirt and trousers he wore were of a dull, earthy hue. But still the man was not ill-looking; rather easy-going and good-natured, I thought.

"Jimini!" he now said to us, "I guess the boss is concarnin' hisself 'bout things that don't count, no-how. What on earth has it to do wid him whether I washes or not? He's sich a crank on soap and wather! It's a waste of time, sez 1 to him when he gets jawing. I reckon a wash every three days in hot weather in them parts is plenty good enough for any respectable man, an' once a week in winter, when it's maybe ten below zero. What d'ye think, mates?"

I think Pete must have been meant by nature for the diplomatic service, for he replied that every man was supposed to know best what was good for himself. It was probably, he explained, a matter of early training. He was afraid, speaking for his friend—myself—and himself, that we had been rather recklessly brought up, for we had contracted the rather unfortunate habit of wasting a good deal of time, not to speak of good soap and water, in washing ourselves.

"You must be precious dirty blokes!" remarked Jim, thoughtfully. "It's them as is clean who don't require to wash. Whoever heerd of a clean man hevin' to wash hisself?"

I came to the conclusion that Jim's mental calibre was of a delightfully original nature, if it did take a somewhat unpleasant turn so far as the prejudices of his comrades were concerned. Pete merely remarked that there was a good deal in what he said, and showed a disposition to change the subject. Jim rose from the up-turned keg on which he had seated himself, and for the first time I realised what a burly giant the man was.

"Now thin, gintlemin," he observed, "I guess grub-pile's about a fair thing. Jist walk ahead of me, if you don't mind, out of that there door or the boss is sure to come down wallop. He's been gettin' precious cranky of late — a-goin' bahmy on the crumpet, I reckon."

We made no comments upon his rather un-guarded remarks but thought that what he said was extremely likely. Pete and I passed together out of the doorway and entered the kitchen indicated. Pierre, who was a French-Canadian, and a dapper, middle-aged, shrewd-looking fellow, made a little bow as we entered, which Pete and I at once acknowledged by removing our hats—a proceeding which seemed to intensely amuse Jim—and took our seats at the table which the cook pointed out to us.

"Gentlemen," Pierre said with a politeness that seemed to me misplaced, "pray be seated, and I shall endeavour your requirements to meet."

I thanked him, and asked if I could assist him in any way. This mutual exchange of civilities seemed to grate on Jim's susceptibilities.

"Borack!" he grunted, "you're not in the Windsor Hotel at Montreal now, Froggy. What hev' you got to eat?—thet's the main point. Black-tail steak! Well, I guess them steaks be sufficiently done for any Christian—you knows I likes mine half raw, I does. See here—"

Without asking the cook's permission he lifted the grill from the wood fire with the evident intention of tossing the steaks with his dirty fingers into a tin dish that stood on the table. With a look of horror and indignation on his face, and with his black beady eyes protruding from their sockets, Pierre caught hold of the grill with one hand and Jim's right hand with the other.

"Mon Dieu!" he exclaimed, "what on earth you do? You are an extremely dirty fellow! You will be good enough to seat yourself and I will myself serve. Your manners remind me of the pig-sow!"

And to my no little surprise the little cook wrested the grill—which was merely an ingenious contrivance of fence wire—from the hands of the in no way abashed giant, and pushed him into his seat opposite us. It was quite evident the cook was in no way apprehensive of reprisal.

"I reckon, you've got much the same silly notions as the boss, Pierre," remarked Jim resentfully, "but I bears no malice—" He looked at and addressed us—" He's a queer chap, Pierre, he be: a washin' of hisself three bloomin' times a day and eatin' of frogs and snails—Faugh! some people be mortal dirty and disgustin' and no mistake!"

Pierre merely shrugged his shoulders as if in .contempt, and proceeded to dish up the dinner, while our jailor placed his two brown hands upon the table in front of him and regarded them admiringly. Pete suggested to me afterwards that probably he wished to spoil our appetites so as to have all the more food for himself.

I was surprised at the quality and variety of the food placed before us. There were deer-steaks, and cold bear's meat which I considered excellent; eggs, good potatoes, spinach, yeast bread, fresh butter and cheese. Pierre also offered us a little whiskey and water. We thanked him, but declined the whiskey and took some tea instead. If we were to escape we would have to keep our heads always clear so as to seize our opportunity. Pierre eventually joined us in our meal, which proceeded in harmony, Jim's mouth being generally too full to speak, save when he had finished what was on his plate and was obliged to ask for more.

"Now, them eggs," remarked Broncho Pete to Pierre, in whose good graces he seemed anxious to stand, "if it's a fair question, where did you get them? You ain't got no cocks and hens here so far as I kin see."

"Ah, non!" exclaimed the little fat cook, "and it is no cocks and hens we do want here. The crowing of a cock in the morning one would hear for miles; we get them as we get most other things—when we delivered our cargoes have, and otherwise would empty-handed be. But we a good garden cultivate on the island. I think it would amuse you to work in it while you are here."

I told Pierre it would give me very great pleasure indeed to do so. After dinner, Pete and I, unasked, assisted him to clean up the dinner things, which simple office seemed to find favour in his eyes. Then we were marched back to an empty shed where we seated ourselves on an old tarpaulin spread on the ground

My companion smoked while I watched Jim, who some paces off had seated himself on the mud floor, and with his back to a post, and with his pipe in his mouth, watched us fitfully with eyes that every now and again closed as if in sleep, only to open as suddenly again and to glare at us apprehensively. The rest of the smugglers were evidently resting, for a deep stillness brooded over the little island. The sun beat down on the lake with a fierce white heat, and the shadows lay black as jet, cleanly cut, palpable. Our surroundings seemed steeped in an air of unreality. It took an effort of will to realise that we were prisoners on a lonely island, the haunt of smugglers and desperadoes, in an almost inaccessible and mythical lake—the dread Lake of the Lost Spirits. How well that sheet of water was named, for surely Pete and I were now well lost to the world. Then I caught myself wondering how long it would be before my uncle and Colin Dunbar would forget that such an unimportant person as myself had ever crossed their paths.

And Muriel Wray; it was odd that a girl should enter into my thoughts at all; but she was something more to me than a mere girl; she had been a friend to me in the truest sense of the word, she had been so good and taken such an interest in me; why, goodness only knew, for I realised that in the knowledge of most things she was my superior. Would she soon forget me? I hoped not. If she did, and by some occult process I were to become aware of it, that, I thought, would be the most distressful phase of the situation. And the twenty pounds she had lent me? It galled me to think that I had not paid it back. To anyone with a spark of honour in him, debt ought to be the greatest menace to peace of mind. Truly my schemes to get on in the world seemed doomed to be shelved for an indefinite period. The thought of this enforced idleness was almost unbearable.

"Pete," I whispered to my companion, "what do you think about it? Have you got any idea in your head as to how we can get out of this?"

"I'm a-thinkin', Wally, I'm a-thinkin'," he replied, puffing hard at his pipe and with a far-away look in his eyes, "it'll be a precious hard thing to do to get out of this 'ere place, seeing as how we're allus pretty sure to be watched. Them two boats are certain to be kept so it'll be impossible for us to get at them. If we do break that there dunjin-cell—where we're safe to be clapped in every night—it would have to be a raft. We must take stock of the material for it, and what logs we can lay our hands on through the day, so that we can put 'em together quickly during the night. But I'm afraid we may hev' to wait days and weeks before we gets our chance."

"I've just got an idea, Pete," I remarked. "Wouldn't it be a good thing if we could only send word to our friends or the police and let them know our whereabouts?"

Pete looked at me sharply, and then, I thought, with pity, as if he suspected I had taken leave of my senses.

" I'm afeard, Wally; I'm afeard," he remarked gently, " you see, there's no Royal Mail in them parts, and as that feller Kippler sez in his song : 'There ain't no buses runnin' twixt the Bank and Mandalay.' No, Wally, old stocking, that won't cotton on, and as for bribing one o' them chaps to carry a message, they knows such a thing would mean death if discovered. No, thet won't do neither."

" Easy, Pete, of course I know that. What I thought of doing was to write a few notes and stick them into bottles and slip them into the lake ; they would in all probability drift on to the mainland if the wind was in the right direction, and the chances are that some search party would pick them up on the beach. I've read of people in books and in the newspapers doing such things."

"Bully for you, pardner! bully for you!" whispered Pete admiringly. "There's lots o' bottles lying round, and I think the sooner we does it the better. But you'll hev' to do the writin' part, as bein' last at school; broncho-bustin' and the three R's ain't got much in common."

As luck would have it I carried a tiny note-book in my belt, which they had not thought of taking from me. It had been part of my work on the round-up to keep tally of all the cattle

branded, and it had been used by me to do so.
Jim still kept but a half-wakeful look-out upon
our actions. It was an easy matter to write out
these notes. I did so at once and placed them
in the lining of my hat for fear of accidents.
We furtively secured some corks, and managed
to hide a flat pint bottle apiece in the bulgy
folds of our shirts. Luck was in our way, for
before dark we had managed to launch a couple
of messages on the Lake of the Lost Spirits
without any particular trouble.

Being late in the fall of the year the days were
short and night came on apace. We had supper
with Pierre and Jim as before, and then were
taken to our prison-house for the night. I
confess my heart sank within me when I saw it.
It was the dread dungeon-cell the strange-man-
nered smuggler-chief had spoken about.

CHAPTER XVI.

IN CAPTIVITY.

OUR resting place for the night was simply a
large, dry species of cave in the precipitous
rock that guarded the island on two sides.
Advantage had been taken of a large hollow
running up from the beach, and along the face of
the cliff, to build a wall on the lake side until it
was converted into a species of long gallery.
This had doubtless been used by the smugglers
before they grew bolder and built the large
wooden huts which they now occupied. At the
far end, and high above our heads in the side
of the wall, was a little window with an iron bar
running across it let into the stone-work. Some
twenty feet or so beneath it we could hear the lap
of the water against the foot of the cliff. It would
be next to impossible to escape that way. At the
lower end of the gallery, screened on the outside
by a dense undergrowth of wolf-willow, was a
massive door, hung by heavy iron hinges to
what seemed undressed door-posts of pine. It
seemed made to stand a siege. Kegs and cases
and empty bottles were strewed about every-

where. At the far end were two piles of dried grass on which a pair of blankets had been flung. These were to be our respective beds.

Our jailor Jim, who had lit a candle which was thrust in the neck of an empty bottle, waited until we had divested ourselves of such garments as we thought could be dispensed with under the circumstances. Pete and I had somewhat fallen in his good opinion, because we had expressed a desire to wash ourselves in the lake before turning in. At first the man, who seldom required to wash, had pretended not to hear our entreaties, but when he found he could no longer ignore them, he gave way with a show of resignation that testified to the intensity of his feelings. He marched to where he and his comrades slept, and from under his palliasse produced what seemed to be a dirty linen rag of a dull brown hue, and a tiny piece of what looked like some kind of fossilised sandstone, but which he assured us was actually soap. He handed them to Pete, who received them with apparent gratitude and show of thanks. But with a twinkle in his eye the treacherous cowboy handed them to me.

"Wally, old stocking," the cunning wretch remarked, "thy necessity be greater than mine!"

"I couldn't think of robbing you, Pete," I hastened to say. "Age before beauty, you know!"

"Waal, you two jokers are queer cusses,"

observed Jim, who had been listening to this interchange of courtesies, " putting such a valee on sich-'like fal-de-rals. To tell 'e the truth I seldom uses them things. Thet towel has been under thet mattress for three months and more. When I washes I either uses my shirt to dry myself wid, or let's the blessed hatmosphere do it instead; it's a way thet saves time and trouble and costs nought."

Fortunately just then Alan the smuggler entered the hut, took in the situation at a glance, went to a large chest, and taking out a couple of rough, clean towels and half a bar of soap handed them to us.

" Here," he remarked somewhat gruffly as I thought, and without almost looking at us, " you better freeze on to these."

It was then, on going down to the lake to wash, that we had seized our opportunity to slip the bottles containing the messages into the water round a bend of the rock, to find an uncertain haven.

When we had lain down on our rude beds, Jim put out the light and took his departure, with the intimation that it was useless trying to make any attempt at escape, as a certain daring officer of the law had been confined in that same cell for over six months, and though he had managed to provide himself with tools, had failed to break his prison. No one, he warned us, could possibly profit by our attempt at escape but the fishes in the lake.

Moreover, we were liable to be visited at any hour of the night by one of our captors.

When he had gone, and we were left in darkness, save for the shaft of moonlight that shone in through the narrow window above our heads, I asked Pete what he thought had become of the prisoner Jim had referred to.

"I dunno," he replied thoughtfully. "Guess it must hev' bin a pretty smart chap called Dunthorne, a corporal in the Mounted Police. He was an enterprisin' daring feller and was in charge of Willow Creek detachment. He was rather fond of wandering into all them wild parts all by hisself, although it was against orders for any man to go out alone. One day he went out and niver came back, and although the whole country was scoured, no trace of him has been found to this day. There was some people as said as he had deserted across the lines, but it's only the worst characters in the police as does that—and there's nothing put in their way to prevent 'em doing it—niver a good man as was Dunthorne. Now, I fancies that poor chap came to an untimely end in this yere show. If so, we'll find out the truth somehow or other, and Mister blooming Campbell or whoiver done it 'll have to answer to a pretty heavy charge-sheet."

This was not a pleasant outlook for us, but we discussed the situation, and what probable chances there were of escape, until, tired out in body and in mind, we both fell fast asleep.

M

We awoke at break of day feeling rather chilly, for as it was now the end of October we had already experienced some sharp frosts.   As there were no signs of anyone approaching, Pete allowed me to mount on to his back and shoulders as he stood against the wall, and I reconnoitred through the narrow window.   But I could see nothing save the cold, blue waters of the lake gleaming far below, a neighbouring island or two crested with shapely pine trees, and the great, sombre cliff of the Lake of the Lost Spirits looming up in the background like the Titanic prison walls they assuredly were. My heart sank within me as I realised the almost insurmountable obstacles that would have to be overcome before we could make our escape.   The Prisoner of Chillon was not more handicapped.

"It's no use, Pete," I remarked somewhat glumly, on descending from my companion's shoulders, " but I've got an idea.   There's lots of bottles here and we can write a few messages, cork them up, and chuck them out of the window.   There's a light breeze blowing that will carry them to the eastern shore."

No sooner said than done, and within the next few minutes we had throw three messages out of the window.   We were somewhat apprehensive lest the bottles might not get clear of the island before some of the smugglers were afoot, for should any of them be seen by our captors it was hard to say what revenge they might not take upon us for our enterprise. In about an hour's time we heard the key turn in the massive lock at the lower end of the gallery, and the door was thrown open to admit our jailer of the previous day.

"Now then, mates," he drawled leisurely—he somehow gave one the idea of a chronic tiredness, and of doing things in a half-hearted way—"show a leg there. Froggy's up, and grubpile's nigh ready. Waal you are queer jokers to tek off your togs when you turn into bed of a night—jest like the rest of them! What's the blooming use, sez I, to tek off one's boots and clothes when one has to put them on agen in the morning. Most people are so cranky in sich things."

We did not contradict him, believing as we did that to let him ventilate freely his unclean and original views was a matter of sound policy.

When we prepared to leave the gallery Jim noticed that we carried towels and soap in our hands.

"I say, mates," he broke out, eyeing us resentfully, "you don't mean to tell me you 'er agoin' to wash yourselves agen!—you washed yourselves last night!—thet should last you for quite a while."

Pete explained to him that as we had unfortunately contracted the bad habit of having a cold bath every morning he was afraid of disastrous effects if we broke it off all at once. It was, he said, like a man who had been in the habit of taking a good deal of liquor, and who was called upon suddenly to give it up entirely. It was necessary in such a case to ease off gradually.

This home truth seemed to appeal to Jim's sympathies, and on assuring him that we would only dive into the lake and out again, he led us down to a large flat rock where there was deep water alongside. When we took that dive I noticed he held his revolver conveniently in one hand. But he need not have done so, for that dip, though wonderfully refreshing, dissipated at once any half-formed scheme we may have had of swimming ashore, the water was so deadly, icily cold. No one could have stayed in it for more than three minutes without getting cramp.

At breakfast we learned that Campbell, the ruffian called Bill, Alan, and the Indian, had gone overnight with a boat's load of contraband goods. Pete explained to me during the course of the day, that he thought the lake narrowed to the north, ran in a narrow canyon far into the mountains, and that at its extreme end it was more than likely the smugglers were met by confederates with pack-horses, who transferred the goods from the boats, and took them by means of some tortuous bridle-track up through the dense pine forests and across the Cypress Hills. Doubtless some ostensible farmer on the Plains of Promise was in league with them, and took the liquor in wagons covered with farming produce, into the little villages that here and there fringed the great Canadian Pacific Railway. As we afterwards discovered, this was indeed the *modus operandi*.

After breakfast, during which the usual wordy warfare took place between the fastidious Pierre and our incorrigible jailor, we were marched for a hundred yards through the pines until we came to quite a trim little kitchen-garden alongside a miniature bay. It struck us as somewhat odd to see such a well-kept, homely spot, filled with the flowers and plants we knew so well, in the stronghold of a band of desperadoes. Pierre came, pointed out to us that a certain plot of ground had to be cleared of certain old stumps and dug over, then left us again to be overlooked by our leisurely jailer. We were supplied with the necessary tools for our task, and, cn it being hinted that we need not break our necks over it, began operations.

It was not much of a task, and, as under the circumstances it would have been folly to over-exert ourselves, we made a pleasant recreation of what otherwise might have been convict's work. Our jailor tilted up a rough wheelbarrow on end where he could command a good view of us, and seating himself safely on it, promptly went to sleep. I suggested to Pete that we should take advantage of his condition, secure his revolver, and make him our prisoner; but Pete was a man who weighed contingencies. He said that, at that very moment, leaving

Pierre out of the question, the sixth ruffian of the gang might be watching us from some point of vantage with a rifle in his hands awaiting an excuse to shoot us down. We must make certain of success before making a move.

It was a lovely, bright, clear day—a typical "Indian summer's" day. The dark blue waters of the lake shimmered in the sunlight, and a number of hawks, poising on balanced pinion far above our heads, gave life and animation to the scene. Against our little bay on a neighbouring island, where trees other than pine grew, the dense foliage was one great blaze of rich and varied colouring. There is no place in the world where Mother Nature shows such gorgeous tints in the fall of the year as in Canada. Here olive greens, reds, yellows, and bronzes glowed side by side, like mighty gems set in a bed of turquoise.

Our task completed we seated ourselves on a log right in front of the sleeping smuggler and waited for him to awake.

"Ain't he a beauty?" Pete remarked admiringly, as with a twinkle in his duty eye he surveyed the great shock of hair that stood up from the walnut-hued face, the long matted beard, and the wide open mouth. To these charms were added a nasal accompaniment that would have made a professional bag-pipe player turn green with envy.

"Don't be jealous, Pete," I observed. "If Providence has been kind and given him greater physical advantages than yourself, you shouldn't——"

But I did not finish the sentence, for Pete began one of his peculiar mirthless cackles, and gave me such a dig in the ribs that I lost my balance, and tilted backwards over the log. In the confusion that followed the sleeping beauty awoke.

"What-ho!" he exclaimed glaring at us stupidly. "I guessed as how that washin' would get into your brains. Crikey, if I wasn't nigh goin' to sleep! Must be close on grub-pile I guess, so let's go to the kitchen."

He arose, stretched himself like a great dog, never so much as looked to see whether we had completed our task or not, and pointed the way to the huts. In the kitchen we found Pierre and the other two smugglers who doubtless had been engaged all the morning in their illegal operations. The party being such a small one it had been decided that we should all have the mid-day meal together. As Pete and I were desirous of washing our hands before sitting down to dinner, and not caring to court the displeasure of our jailer further by our fastidious predilections, we covertly showed the condition of our hands to Pierre, whereupon the little man stormed and gesticulated and packed the three of us down to the lake-side to wash. Jim grumbled and commented forcibly on the degenerate condition of those who were obliged to clean themselves two or three times a day. He dipped his own hands gingerly into the water, with obvious repugnance, and then rubbed them dry on his dirty mole-skin trousers.

At dinner we found that the two smugglers with whom we had not before been brought directly in contact were remarkably silent and taciturn.   At the same time it was quite evident that little escaped their notice, and that they were very wide-awake indeed.   They had a trick of avoiding one's eyes, and furtively watching one when they thought they were not observed.   At any unwonted sound, one of them would rise apprehensively, draw his revolver from its pouch and go outside.   One thing I noticed during our stay on the island, was that no one ever went about without fire-arms.   This was a precaution which had grown out of that vision of a scaffold—or more likely a tree with a rope and a noose—the ever-menacing Nemesis of black unpunished crime.

We assisted 'n the washing-up after dinner, and then were locked up in the gallery for an hour or so.   Later on, one of the taciturn smugglers kept us busy in splitting up some large pine logs with iron wedges.   It was while we were thus engaged that a startling incident occurred.   Pete and I had paused for a moment in our labours, when suddenly in the brooding silence, somewhere in the neighbourhood of the cliffs, a couple of rifle shots rang out.   They were immediately followed by the remarkable series of echoes which we had heard on the previous day.

Our jailer started and drew his revolver. Through a vista in the trees we could see the top of the great cliff from which the sounds came. It was the way we had come. We all looked keenly for a moment or two at the pine-fringed ledge without seeing anything. Then several tiny specks like so many ants, appeared upon the brink, and we knew that the rancher, Colin Dunbar, had not gone back to the ranche after all, but alarmed by our absence had taken all the men composing the round-up, and had followed us into the Land of the Lost Spirits to discover our whereabouts. We saw them group together on the brink of the precipice as if scanning the shores of the mysterious lake. Probably the only man who had ever looked upon it before was the rancher himself—the others had doubtless scoffed at the idea of its existence.

Suddenly our jailer gave a peculiar low whistle and covered us with his Colt's.

"Make a move or a sign," he exclaimed "and I'll blow you to Kingdom Come in the twinkling of an eye!"

He looked as if he meant it. In another minute he was joined by the other smugglers and Pierre who had also heard the shots, and at once came hurrying towards us.

For a moment the unexpected idea that help was so near at hand—that we were actually looking upon our would-be deliverers—caused us to forget the imminent and menacing peril of

the smugglers. Our first impulse was to dash
down to the water's edge and try to attract the
attention of our friends. But the sharp click of
the revolvers brought us to our senses.

"It's no use," said the furtive-eyed one, "if
you as much as speak above your breaths, you'll
be both as dead as herrings in two-twos. To
the lock-up with you!"

And next minute we were being marched
towards our prison-cell with three loaded revolvers pointed at our heads. It was a humili-
ating position to be in, but it would have been
madness to have made a move.

CHAPTER XVII.

A MYSTERIOUS FRIEND.

WE were not allowed out of the gallery again that day, our evening meal being brought in to us. At intervals we could hear far-off, hollow-sounding rifle shots, with their accompanying remarkable series of echoes pealing out as the round-up party separated, and went off in opposite directions to search the shores of the lake. Pete and I wondered if any of our bottles containing the messages had managed to make the required distance to the shore, and get stranded on the narrow strip of beech which showed in some places. This we very much doubted. If a message did fall into the hands of the cowboys, then our rescue was assured. The cowboys would simply construct a large raft in some sheltered nook, and bearing down upon the island in the night, simply take the place by storm. The smugglers would hardly have time to wreak their vengeance upon us. We could easily secure the door so that they could not open it in case of contingencies. But it was galling and maddening to think that our friends were so near at hand, and yet quite unconscious of our presence. More than likely the idea of our being on any of the islands never for one moment suggested itself. What was there to suggest any such idea !

There was no sleep for us that night. We strained our ears listening for sounds and voices that came not. Several times I mounted on to Pete's shoulders to gaze out of our prison window. But I saw nothing save a broad band of mellow moonlight quivering on the bosom of the lake, and the edge of the high cliff on the western shore silhoutted darkly against the milky ways in the heavens. Where were all my plans for the future now? How was I to make my way in the world if so much precious time was to be wasted fretting my soul out in captivity? It seemed to me as if I had left my boyhood behind, and was at last facing what men called "the stern realities of life."

Next morning our jailers were a long time in showing up, and when they did come they were headed by Campbell, the smuggler-chief, who had doubtless come back with the others in cover of night. His face was as pale and passionless as ever, but his eyes glowed with a light that filled me with an odd fear and apprehension. The man looked positively ill, not only physically, but mentally. Although he was tall he was but sparely built—a mere shadow compared to the burly forms of his associates. But there was that in his eyes which made him a ruler of men:

that which only the possessor of brains and an iron will possesses. He was, doubtless, a man who was meant for better things, but whose fall had perverted and jaundiced his moral and mental outlook. The idea might have been incongruous, but he made me think of the fallen archangel.

He held one hand behind his back as he entered. The two men who were with him had a stern, set expression on their faces. I knew that something extraordinary was about to happen, but what it was, I could not for the life of me make out. In another moment we realised the serious trouble we had got into. He withdrew his hand from behind his back and handed me a scrap of paper torn from my tally book. It was one of the first notes I had put into a bottle and consigned to the waters of the lake. My heart sank within me as I saw it. What revenge would not this mad being resort to now?

"That's your writing, I know," he remarked in a voice that seemed utterly devoid of all feeling. "I congratulate you on your readiness of resource and promptness of action, but it's the old story of theory without experience. You didn't reckon on currents that would carry the bottle right to my very feet in the canyon. You remind me of one of the cleverest boys we ever had at Harrow, who was great on analytical chemistry. He could almost tell you the component parts of any kind of food by merely glancing at it, but he died of starvation afterwards in the Australian bush, with lots of flour and every necessary in his saddle-bags, and close to running water, simply because he hardly knew how to light a fire, far less how to mix flour and water with baking powder and cook it."

"Were you ever at Harrow, sir?" I exclaimed, for the moment forgetting the serious nature of speech in his unpremeditated admission. Something in the man's face seemed to haunt me. But, after all, it was only imagination on my part, I could not possibly have seen him before.

"Never mind," he snapped, "I could see at a first glace you'd been there. What you've got to answer for now is this letter."

"Waal, I guess, Campbell," broke in Pete, "as it's me who's got to answer for thet. It was my idea, and it was me as made him write it, and it was me what slung the bottle overboard."

"I can't believe a single word of what you say, Pete," observed the smuggler, eyeing him calmly. "I am afraid you're too chock full of silly sentiment and romance to live long. Besides, you hadn't the brains to think of such a thing. Some of you cowboys imagine that you're the smartest men on earth, because you never see any people save blamed hobos like yourselves. Bullocks and horses comprise your every-day world; cards and whiskey when you're in town for a holiday.—Bah! if you could only see yourselves as others see you!"

I looked at poor Pete; the blood had mounted into his brown, weather-beaten face, but he did not reply to the unmerited taunts of the man whom he had once saved from death by lynching. It required more moral courage on Pete's part to hold his tongue than to retort. The smuggler continued—

"Now, I'm afraid you two fellows finding your way into these parts has made it very awkward for us, and the chances are that for the next fortnight or so, and until the first fall of snow, the Mounted Police and goodness knows who, will be searching round these parts for your useless bodies, so it will be necessary for all of us to be pretty quiet until they reckon the snow has covered your bones. As to your punishment for trying to give away this establishment, and to bring the red-coats down upon us, I'll think over the matter. There would be little satisfaction in killing you : 'Peace, perfect peace,' won't be yours if I can help it. In the meantime, you'll go without breakfast until you're beyond the necessity of requiring food at all, and I'll see about leg-irons. Bill and you, Jones, make them clean out the gallery. See that every scrap of wood is removed and that there's not a bottle left for them to lay their hands on. Keep a sharp eye on them, and recollect that they're not to leave this for the next fortnight unless they're carried out feet first. Now, Bill, set them to work."

I happened to glance at Pete's face at that

moment and saw that it worked with suppressed feeling. The veins swelled on his forehead and his hands were clasped together convulsively. It was well for us that we still had some measure of self-control left; had we retorted just then, I do not believe our lives would have been worth a minute's purchase.

The smuggler-chief turned on his heel and left; at the same moment Bill ordered us to set to work. I confess it was almost a relief to do something after the tension of the last few minutes. Our head jailor, Bill, and his mate never once spoke to us save to direct our operations. When dinner time came we were glad to sit down, and gladder still to satisfy our healthy appetites, which, to do Pierre justice, he did not neglect; himself bringing us dinner in an old soap box.

That night when we lay down to sleep we were dead tired, and I am afraid that although Pete did his very best to make light of the situation, and to cheer me with his whimsical talk, he was just as down-hearted as myself. Later on there was a sharp frost, and we shivered with cold as we rolled ourselves in our all too scanty blankets. We were glad when daylight struggled in through the narrow casement over our heads, but that day passed much as the other had done. We saw no one save Bill, his mate. and the cook, and when Pete spoke about our blankets having proved insufficient to keep out the cold on the previous night, we were told

with an oath and a sneer that we did not know
when we were well off, for in a short time the
chances were that we would be in a place where
blankets were the very last things we would
want. Towards the afternoon we had cleared
the gallery of everything superfluous, and swept
it out. The enforced idleness that followed was
harder to bear than the enforced toil.

Four days passed and we had never been
allowed outside our cell, save to wash in a
bucket of water that was brought and placed just
outside the doorway. We asked our jailors to
give us something to do so as to break the
deadly monotony of our lives, but they simply
told us that if we wanted a place of entertain-
ment we should not have come to the Land of
the Lost Spirits That night we were startled
by hearing shots fired from the western bank of
the lake, and, seeing a lurid glare in the sky
through the tiny window, I mounted on to Pete's
shoulders, and saw two large beacons burning
on the top of the cliff some cousiderable
distance apart. We knew that these fires were
built by those who were out looking for us. It
was indeed a soul-harrowing thing to know
that we were within sight of our friends, and
that we could do nothing to apprise them of our
presence. If we could only have had a match
or a flint we could have burnt bundles of the
dried grass that constituted the greater part of
our bedding, and the watchers seeing it, would
assuredly have built rafts and searched the

N

islands next day. But Bill and his mate had taken good care to leave us with nothing that could possibly ignite. Unfortunately, from the high cliffs, so thick was the foliage on this the central main island that not a trace of the human habitations it contained could be detected. The smugglers would also be on the *qui vive* so long as they suspected there was any of the search party about. No smoke would betray them now, as it had done on a former occasion to us.

Next morning we had a change of jailors; Alan, the man whose face I thought had borne some hint of pity when he first saw us, and our old friend Jim, who, despite some of his peculiar prejudices, was a decided improvement on the brutal Bill and his taciturn mate. When Alan entered, I confess to having been rather surprised when he did not even vouchsafe us a half-hearted nod, but regarded us sullenly.

"Oh, you're up, are you?" he said. "Jim, go down to the cove for a bucket of water and let them chaps wash themselves. I'll keep my eye and my shooting-stick upon them at the same time."

"Waal, I'm darned!" exclaimed the man, who hated water, with a disgusted look on his face. "Go down and fetch water for them jokers to wash when I wouldn't go the length of my foot to git water for myself! Waal, if you ain't a daisy!"

"All right," remarked Alan coolly, "if you

don't there'll be no quart bottle of whiskey for you 'on the side' when I'm in charge of the spirits."

This fetched Jim, who evidently had at least no prejudice to liquids when in the form of alcohol, for, with a muttered reference to the manners of some people, he picked up a zinc pail and slouched slowly off for the water. The moment he had turned his back a remarkable change came over Alan's face. He turned and scrutinized us keenly.

"Look here," he asked quickly, "are you to be trusted? Honour bright, mind."

"If you don't think we are from what you've seen of us, don't do it," answered Pete.

"Yes, I think you are," said the smuggler. "Here's a book or two for you, Derringham, which I fancy will help you out these days—it's enough to turn a fellow's brain, being cooped up in a shop like this. Hide them somewhere in your blankets. And as for you—Pete, I think the boss called you—here's some baccy; but before I give you matches, will you take a solemn oath never to use them for any other purpose than lighting your pipe?"

"May I never ride another broncho again if I plays you false," said Pete.

"Well, here you are—now, hide them." And the smuggler drew from inside his shirt a couple of Dickens's works and thrust them into my hands. He then took some tobacco and matches from the pouch in his belt and gave them to Pete.

"Quick, get a rustle on," he whispered, looking apprehensively towards the open door.

Somewhat mystified, and with hastily expressed thanks we stowed away the precious articles. They would help us for some time at least to bear up against the deadly monotony of our lives.

"It's awfully good of you to give us these things," I exclaimed gratefully. "Why do you do it? How is it you are with these other men at all?"

For, to put it mildly, there was something about Alan so utterly at variance with his lawless calling, and his obvious goodness of heart, that was puzzling and gave me courage to speak as I did.

"You mustn't ask questions," he replied hastily, but not unkindly. "And look here, you must not mind if I swear at you a bit and treat you roughly before the others, you'll understand it's not meant."

"Say, sonny, whar hev I seen you before?" interrupted Pete, who had been gazing searchingly at our newly-found friend. "First time I clapped eyes on you, blow me if I didn't think I knowed your face."

A look of annoyance clouded the smuggler's countenance, and I thought he changed colour.

I hastened to say—

"Pete, for goodness sake—we've just been told to ask no questions. It's a poor way of paying back a kindness, but I was the first to begin it and I apologize."

"That's right, Derringham," remarked the smuggler, "if you want to keep a friend never inquire too closely into his past. No one cares to parade his family skeleton even for the edification of his friend—its anatomy and the rattling of the bones are liable to be misinterpreted. By the way, did you hear that shooting last night?"

He kept looking towards the doorway anxiously.

"You bet," replied Pete, "and we saw the fires."

"It was the Mounted Police and the cowboys," explained our mysterious friend. "They've been prowling round here these last few days, and I fancy must have explored the Land of the Lost Spirits pretty thoroughly by now."

"It's a wonder they don't get on to some old trail of yours," observed Pete.

"They couldn't," was the quiet reply, "we run the boat into a narrow canyon miles long, into which there's no getting from the top. Then there's an almost subterraneous passage through the mountain that would take a deal of finding. It's much the same at the other end. In a few months from now the world will be welcome to the secret, for the place is getting just a trifle hot for us. But, look here, I've one question to ask you that Campbell seems to have overlooked. Was that message you sent off in a bottle the only one you wrote and put into the lake ? "

Like a lightning flash the idea presented itself to me that here, now, was an explanation of the seeming kindness of the smuggler. He was a mean hypocrite after all, and his attitude towards us was merely assumed for the purpose of finding out our movements and betraying them to his chief. But he did not look like a scoundrel. He had a smart, almost military, appearance, and there was kindliness and strength in his distinctive face, and an honesty in his eyes, that seemed to belie the idea. In another moment I was ashamed of my thoughts, for he had shot a swift glance at me, then turning away said quickly, with what I thought was a note of disappointment in his voice—

" Don't answer, it was natural enough for you to think that. I can hardly expect you to take me on trust."

" I beg your pardon," I rejoined humbly. " We do trust you." I looked at Pete, who nodded. " We have sent four or five messages, but goodness knows whether our friends will get them or not. But if they do, what about you ? They will capture you with the others."

" In that case I've a clearer charge-sheet than most of them," he remarked, with a thoughtful look upon his face. But here's Jim coming up with your water. And, by the way, I know you've been docked of your breakfast and that the other chaps haven't been giving you any.

Now, they forgot to inform me of the fact, so I just told Pierre the cook to let you have it as before; I'll risk the racket."

Pete and I hastily expressed our thanks.

"Now, stand-by," he said cheerfully, "I'm going to give it you hot,"—Jim at that moment entered the cell with the pail. His manner changed in a moment.—"I wish you chaps wouldn't stand there looking as stupid as two owls. Just get a rustle on and polish up your dirty faces. I'll go and fetch breakfast, Jim? while you keep an eye on them. Turn about's fair play."

As he walked quickly off I could not help speculating as to the apparently friendly attitude of the smuggler. Had I not acted imprudently in telling him of those other messages, Was it likely he was going to remain impassive while the chances were one of the bottles might be found at any time, and his capture by the Police follow as a matter of course?

CHAPTER XVIII.

WE ATTEMPT TO ESCAPE.

FOR the next two days Alan and Jim were our jailers which, needless to say, was a pleasant change from the brutal and taciturn espionage from which we had hitherto suffered. For although Alan always addressed us somewhat gruffly before Jim, whenever that gentleman went to sleep—which he invariably did as soon as he had finished his meals—he treated us more like companions than prisoners, and talked with us quite pleasantly. At such times I would take out "David Copperfield" and read, letting Pete, who had a natural antipathy to overtaxing his business eye, carry on the conversation. At night we were locked up and left to ourselves, but as Alan had supplemented our bedding with a couple of pairs of blankets, the rapid lowering of the temperature within the last few days did not disturb us. Strange to say, neither Campbell, the captain of the gang, nor any of the others came near us. I suspected they were keeping a sharp look-out and making preparations for a possible attack. Perhaps Pierre the cook was the most inconvenienced by the presence of the

searchers in the neighbourhood, for he dared
not light a fire of wood lest the smoke should
betray the presence of the smugglers and had to
burn spirit instead.

The suspense and enforced inactivity to which
Pete and I had been subjected was telling upon
us. True, Alan had allowed me to pace up and
down the gallery, and to improvise a pair of
very rough and ready Indian clubs with which I
staved off the horrible feeling of inertia, but
still the sense of being almost within sight of our
friends, and yet knowing that we were so utterly
helpless and at the mercy of the desperadoes, was
mental trouble of a far more trying kind.

Every night had Pete and I discussed the
situation, advancing and abandoning all sorts of
mad schemes by which we might effect an
escape. If something were not done, and that
quickly, those who were searching in the vicinity
for our supposed lifeless bodies must of a necessity give up their quest in despair, seeing that
now considerably over a week had been spent
without any clue to our presence.

At times we were tempted to spring on our
guards unexpectedly, overpower them, secure
their weapons, and make for the little harbour
where the boats lay. But we could not entertain
the idea of stealing a march on Alan who had
been so kind to us, and the others never gave us
a chance. Even had the sleepy Jim been told
off to guard us with a man as sleepy as himself,
and having achieved our purpose to disarm them

we managed to elude the vigilance of the others,
the chances were that the boats were stowed
away in such a manner that we could not make
use of them.   It was a hopeless outlook.
What made the situation to me all the more
annoying, was that doubtless by this time Colin
Dunbar had considered it his duty to communicate with my uncle in England, apprising him of
my dissappearance and my probable fate.   Poor
old uncle Gilbert, I daresay he would regret the
manner of my leaving his house, and be sorry
for me in his own undemonstrative way when
his studies permitted, but very likely the new
family ties he had formed were by this time
occupying more of his attention than he had
bargained for.   I, however, held to the thought
that there was one who would really and truly
be sorry when she heard the news, and that was
my girl friend, Muriel Wray.   Somehow of late
I had been thinking a good deal about her, and
with the broader views of life which I now took,
I wondered at and felt ashamed of the occasions
when I thought it was beneath my dignity to be
seen with her—she who was so good, and so
kind.   It was a mystery to me now how she
could ever have taken any interest in me.
What a young prig I must have been in those
days!   Truly there was nothing like experience and a touch of adversity for taking the
conceit out of one and showing things in their
proper light.   Yes, it was comforting to think .
that there was some human being in whose

heart I would be as a tender memory, for I knew that she had really liked me, and still she was one of the most undemonstrative girls I ever knew.

It was quite plain to us that if we did not make some attempt to attract the attention of our friends, in another day or two it would be too late, and it would be difficult to say what might not become of us. It was imperative that we should make some attempt to escape. Alan had hinted that for the last few days his chief had become still more strange in his manner, and was at times so violent in his behaviour that his comrades stood in considerable apprehension as to their personal safety. He counselled us that should he come to our cell we must not allow ourselves to be provoked into losing our tempers over anything he said. There was no knowing what he might do in such a case.

One day as Pete was watching the tiny patch of blue that showed through the little window over our heads, a half suppressed ejaculation escaped from his lips; he shuffled his feet uneasily, and I knew he had got an idea. We had finished dinner and our guards had gone to theirs, locking us in, so there was nothing to prevent us talking.

"Wally," exclaimed the cowboy, "I guess as how we're two of the blindest bats alive! Do you see that there wall and that window?"

I answered in the affirmative.

"Waal, did it niver strike you that it would be an easy thing to take it to pieces, beginning at the window and working our way down stone by stone. It's only been plastered together with mud, not lime."

To my inexperienced eye the fact had not been apparent. Now it flashed upon me like a revelation with all its possibilities.

"But there's the deep waters of the lake underneath," I said, considering. "And even if we managed to get down to it in safety, how are we to get away?"

"We can drop the stones into the lake until we work down to near the floor, and then we can lower ourselves down by our blankets to the water, an' then it'll only be a few strokes to the shore alongside the doorway. After that it'll be make for the boats, and take our chances in getting clear away."

"To-night, Pete?" I exclaimed.

"Yes, to-night," he replied, " but——"

"Oh, no buts," I interposed. "I'm sick of this, and quite willing to take the risks."

"But I'm not so sure that I'm justified in lettin' you take 'em. I'm older than you, Wally, and hev had a good innings, so if I should get bowled out it wouldn't so much matter, but you——"

"Pete," I expostulated, " it doesn't matter about me so much as you think. I'm pretty well alone in the world, and I'd rather die trying to do something to help myself than remain here at the mercy of a mad smuggler and his men. As likely as not they may at any moment

discover that our lives seriously compromise
their own safety, and that it would be better to
end these lives without a moment's warning.
I'm eating my heart out in this place. Besides,
I don't see what is to prevent us escaping. If
they have got the boats locked up, I don't see why
we can't fix up a raft from some of the logs and
boxes lying about and drift and paddle ashore."

"All right, Wally, if you're willing to take
chances. You're not a chicken now, and a'most
as big as a man. Can you swim?"

I assured him of the fact, so we at once began
to discuss our risky project.

As we knew our jailors would not be back for
another half-hour or so, I assumed my position
on Pete's shoulders, and examined the casement, so as to determine the best way of beginning operations when it grew dark. I discovered
that it would be by no means an impossible
task. When once the thick plastering of mud
was removed, the blocks of basalt would not be
difficult to detach from one another. For some
reason or other I had hidden the strong stave of
a cask in my bedding, and that might come in
handy to use as a lever. If only the slight
breeze that had sprung up continued, there
would not be so much danger of the smugglers
hearing the stones drop into the lake. We
more than suspected that two or three times
during the night one or other of the smugglers
came and examined the door of the gallery, but
the chances were that this inspection would not

extend further. As for Alan, we had both grown to like the man whose one seeming antipathy was to talk about himself. He had evidently received a good education, and with the exception of his chief, belonged to a very different order of beings from his mates. We knew he was sorry that we had fallen into their hands, but we also knew that if some of the others suspected his sympathies were with us, and that there was any danger of him conniving at our escape, his life would not be worth a moment's purchase. We would have liked to tell him of our intentions, but we thought it was more than likely it would only place him in a most unpleasant predicament. It was a mystery to us how a quiet, kindly, evidently right-thinking man should have come to cast in his lot with a gang of desperadoes. Since that time I have seen so many extraordinary phases of life that I have ceased to wonder at anything.

It was only with difficulty we could conceal our suppressed excitement from the two men who kept guard over us that afternoon, but at last the long day came to an end. It was with an inexpressible feeling of relief that we heard the great key turn in the lock, and the great pine bar put into its place and wedged home. We had carefully examined that door on the first night of our imprisonment, and realised that it was useless trying to tamper with it.

The night was cold and dark, the moon was

on the wane, and as we knew it would not rise till midnight, we delayed operations till then. It was as well we did so, for just as we noted that a wan ray of moonlight had struggled in through the narrow casement, and we were about to rise from our beds, we heard the scuffling of feet outside, the removing of the heavy bar, and the turning of the key in the lock. In another moment three men entered. They closed the door behind them, struck a light and lit a candle which one of them held in his hand. I could see by its dim light that one of them was Campbell, another the brutal Bill, and the third the seemingly ill-mated Alan. Campbell was in his shirt-sleeves, his face was of a ghastly pallor, and his eyes were wild and glassy. In one hand he held a large Colt's revolver. It was quite evident to me that either the man was suffering from the effects of drink, or else he had passed the stage of incipient madness. The smugglers had never visited us like this before in the middle of the night. What was their reason for doing so now? That it was for no good it was not difficult to divine. Instinctively Pete and I drew the blankets close up to our chins, and feigned to be sound asleep. But still it was an unpleasant thing to think that we were so utterly at the mercy of that mad wretch with the cocked revolver in his hand. The three men came quietly enough towards us, and we knew that they were holding the light so as to see whether we were asleep or not. Both Pete and I breathed heavily, the former indeed supplementing his part by something that resembled a nasal note. Suddenly something occurred that required all my powers of self-control to keep me from crying out and springing to my feet. Campbell had made a movement, and someone, whom I guessed by his voice was Alan, had stayed his hand in some attempted action.

"Don't do any such silly trick," said our smuggler friend, with a temerity for which I had hardly given him credit. "A lot of satisfaction there is in potting a sleeping man and a youngster! I wonder you're not jolly well ashamed of yourself."

"Let me go, you squeamish fool!" hissed the desperado. "You don't seem to realise that if it wasn't for these born idiots we shouldn't be surrounded by a troop of Mounted Police and all the cowboys in the country at the present moment. The powers of darkness take them! It's only a question of time now before they're exploring these islands on the ice, and the game will be up. In the meantime it's as much as our necks are worth to attempt to run a cargo up the canyon. Oh, curse them! I must be even with them! I'll have a fit unless I put a bullet through their brains!"

"You'll have something else if you don't look out. What right have you to put us all in a hole for the sake of gratifying your bloodthirsty notions of revenge? You seem to have lost your head completely of late. Why not keep them

here as sort of hostages, so that, should the
police find out our whereabouts, you could tell
them that unless they allowed you to clear safely
out of the country you would at once do them up.
There would be more sense in that."

"Yes, boss, I guess that's not a bad idea,"
growled Bill, who, like most brutal men, had a
very tender regard for his own personal well-
being. "That's the ticket! When the red-
coats come round, you jest hev' them two blokes
a sittin' on a nice little keg of gunpowder, where
they kin see 'em. You stand at the business end
of the fuse, and sez you, ' is it a clear trail for us
chaps or is it Kingdom Come for them?' The
chances are they'll tell us to show our heels. If
they don't, then you can fire the fuse and intro-
duce them jokers to the angels. There would be
some fun in that."

Pete and I hardly thought so, but we hoped
that Campbell would listen to the tender-hearted
Bill's advice. In another moment we found that
it had found favour in his eyes.

" That's not a bad idea, Bill," he said, " and
the effect would be quite dramatic. I'm blowed
if I wouldn't mind being shot after it merely for
the pleasure of seeing these two fellows going up
in little pieces to join the stars. Come on, let's
go. I'll have another drink before I turn in so's
to send me to sleep. They'll be all right till
morning."

When they had gone and closed the door
behind them, Pete and I sprang to our feet with

O

inexpressible relief. There were no doubts or hesitation as to what we should do. The sooner we were out of the clutches of such a truly diabolical crew the better. If we were killed in attempting to escape we would be no worse off. I groped my way to the door and picked up a box of matches that Campbell had inadvertently placed on a small shelf and forgotten, when he had lighted the candle. They would come in handy, and save Pete from breaking his word with Alan about the matches he had got from him. Besides I had a project to attract the attention of any of the search-party who might yet be on the mainland.

I took the stave, and mounted on to Pete's shoulders.

"Now, Wally," said my cheery friend, "smash the plaster up, then try and lever out some of them there stones. When oncet you've made a beginning I'll git up and help."

I set to work with right good will. In less than ten minutes I had removed the mud-plaster and discovered the first vulnerable part in the stone-work. It was with a feeling of joy and exultation that I pushed my first stone out through the narrow window and heard it rebound from the rocks and splash into the lake beneath. Then my blood ran cold with sudden fear; what if the smugglers should hear the noise? But the wind had fortunately freshened, and the breaking of the little waves against the cliff would surely deaden the sound of the falling débris. I scraped and tugged away at the stones with my hands until there was hardly a whole inch of skin on them, but soon I had the pleasure of loosening the four large stones that constituted the casement of the window, and pushing them one by one into the lake. Then I worked downwards, and the rest was comparatively easy work. In an hour's time I had made a hole almost large enough to stand upright in, but Pete insisted on me taking a rest, so I climbed down and he took my place. Very soon he informed me that now we might risk the lake. The soft mellow moonlight streamed in through the great gap we had made in the wall and flooded our cell. By its light we tore our blankets into long strips, which Pete skilfully and quickly converted into a long rope. By means of the stave we made one end of it fast in the stone-work, letting the other dangle over the ledge outside.

And now the time had come for us to entrust our bodies to the icy waters of The Lake of the Lost Spirits.

CHAPTER XIX.

THE PURSUIT.

PETE clambered on to the partially demolished wall and peeped into the gloomy depths below.

"It's a long way down, Wally," he observed, "but the rope's nigh touching the water. I'll go first, and you follow me up. Here goes."

He took hold of the rope, and with his foot braced against the cliff, began to lower himself down. When he had disappeared from view I took his place on the wall and watched him, as, hand over hand, he gradually neared the cold, black water. It must have been at least thirty feet from where I knelt to its surface. Pete must have been close to it, when suddenly, to my surprise, he stood upright, felt about with his feet, relaxed his hold on the rope, and steadied himself against the face of the cliff with his hands. He looked up towards me and cried—

"Come on, Wally, I believe I've struck a ledge!"

In two minutes more I stood by his side. It was indeed a ledge, but an exceedingly narrow one. By closely hugging the cliff we could just get a foothold, and no more. It sloped gradually shorewards. When we stepped from it on to the firm sand of the beach, my teeth were chattering in my head, and I hardly knew whether my nether limbs belonged to me or not, for the last several yards of our progress had been through water which reached to our knees. I never in my life found water so icily cold. It made me shudder to think of what total immersion in it would have meant.

"Now then, Wally, we'll have to make for the boats," whispered Pete. "I reckon the best thing to do would be to crawl along the shore in the shadow. If you see or hear anything move, lie as still as death. It's do or die this time."

The waning moon shed but a feeble light upon the deep cliff-encircled lake and the lonely islands nestling on its bosom. I noted how within the last few days the frost had brought down the leaves, causing the boughs to show like fine filigree work or tracery against the star-lit heavens. The light breeze made an eerie sound among the pines and the honey-combed rocks. How cold and cheerless the dark waters looked as they broke against the inhospitable, jagged rocks! I wondered if in all God's earth there could be another spot so weirdly desolate and set apart as this.

But there was no time for thinking about such things. What we had to do was to secure the boats and leave the island. If we did not succeed in doing so it meant certain death for us in the morning—perhaps before then if we were discovered. My nerves were in a painful state of tension. When some large night-bird like a great grey spirit swooped past over our heads, cleaving the air with its razor-like wings, and uttering a harsh, loud cry which resembled that of some human being in pain, my heart stood still with sudden fright, and then fluttered fitfully.

We crawled along the rocky shore in the shadow of the banks, every now and again pausing to listen and peer in the deceptive semi-darkness. How every tree-stump and rock seemed to resolve themselves into some sinister, lurking enemy. Every moment I almost expected to see a little tongue of fire spurt out from the gloom presaging the deadly leaden messenger, or to be challenged in a rough voice by someone on the watch.

But at last we reached the little natural harbour and turned into it with a world of dread and apprehension in our hearts. What if the boats had been carried well ashore, or rendered useless for our purpose? There would then be nothing for it but to search for some logs or spars, lash them together, and trust ourselves to their frail support. But the boats were there, made fast to the little jetty, and there was exultation in our hearts as we fairly ran down to them. And then, O horrible sense of disappointment and dismay as we discovered they were both securely chained to a huge pile driven into the sand, with the great padlock in such a position that we could not get at it so as to spring the lock by the usual means adopted in such cases — by dealing it heavy blows with large stones.

"Wally, old stocking," whispered Pete, "it's a blue look-out. But we musn't waste time. Let's look for some logs—anything at all; it won't do to stop round this 'ere shop long. They may discover that we've cleared out any minute."

It was indeed a tantalising sight to see the two boats lying there so trimly side by side, with the oars in them, and still so utterly useless for our purpose. But my old faculty of observation once more stood me in good stead.

"Pete," I said, "I believe I know where they keep the key of that padlock. It is kept hung up on a nail in the still-house at the far end of the building. I once saw Jim put it there."

"Are you quite sure it was the key of this padlock?" asked Pete.

"I'm almost sure of it," I replied; "at least, it was the key of a padlock —you can always tell the difference. You just stop here and I'll go and get it."

Pete wanted to go himself, averring that he knew the ground better than I did, but I would not have it. The suggestion and project were mine, and mine would be the risk.

"You run as much risk of being shot, Pete, by staying here," I declared. "I'm going, so it's no use your trying to persuade me to the contrary. I can lay my hands on that key I'm pretty certain, and should even the smugglers happen to hear me I can get back again before they can make out what's up. You stand by and be ready to help me. So long, old chap."

I hastily shook him by the hand and was off before he could prevent me or say a word. The still-house was the farthest away of the log huts, so I skirted the hollow among the pines in order to enter it by the doorway at the back. It was dark in the shadow and I stumbled against rocks and tree-stumps. Every little noise brought my heart into my mouth, for I thought the smugglers must necessarily hear it, and I knew that meant certain death for both Pete and myself. Still, I will say this for myself, that it was not so much the actual fear of death that concerned me as the failure or mismanagement of the mission which I had taken upon myself, and upon which the life of another hung.

I crouched and crept along as best I could until I stood on the top of the lip of the little hollow just behind the still-house. Everything seemed perfectly quiet and the huts had a deserted appearance. There was a light breeze blowing, and one or two loose boards on a ruined shed flapped eerily to and fro. I looked across the dim lake to the south where the shadow of the mighty western cliff lay like a great eclipse athwart the dim waters, clearly defined, black as jet, palpable. Suddenly from the blackness there gleamed out a light so intensé, so bright, that for a moment it fairly dazzled me. It lit up the weird gulch of waters as if the sun were blazing directly overhead, and the vast cliffs with every tree and scar stood out distinctly. But the cause of that flash itself I could not determine. It was of such infinitesimal duration that but for the sudden affright of the bird-world I could have almost fancied myself the victim of some optical illusion. What weird phenomenon of nature was this?

But there was no time to lose in idle speculation, and I turned at once to the hut. Quickly I walked over the intervening clear ground. Luckily the door stood wide open, and I stepped inside. It was pitch dark, and owing to the number of formidable obstacles, mostly in the form of tubs and jars, littering the floor, I nearly broke my neck in trying to get to the spot where the key was kept. I would never get there without a light of some kind. The noise caused by my tumbling about would be more likely to be heard than any light employed for a minute or two was likely to be seen. If the key was to be found one would have to take risks in finding it. I struck a wax vesta and made my way quickly to where the key was kept. Thank goodness, there it was, and hastily I secured it. I was now close to the door when suddenly the match burnt my fingers, and hastily I threw it from me. In another second a great tongue of flame shot up from an open keg close to the wall, and in another moment it seemed

as if the whole place was ablaze. Some kind of
oil or spirit must have been left uncovered and
my match had done the business. For a
moment I stood helpless, incapable of thought
or action. To try and stop the progress of that
fierce flame would be a fatuous task; turning, I
dashed across the space of open ground and by
the way I had come. That hut burned as if it
had been made of tissue paper soaked in kero-
sene. The breeze fanned the flames through the
doors and windows with almost incredible
rapidity; there was a series of loud reports as
jars and kegs of spirit were exploded by the
fierce heat, and before I had reached the little
harbour immense forks of blue flames and red
were shooting through the roof. Glancing over
my shoulder I could see the smugglers rushing
out of their hut evidently in a great state of
consternation. Would it serve to distract their
attention while we made our escape? If so,
then the dropping of that match was a fortuitous
accident.

"Quick, Pete," I cried, almost breathless,
handing him the key. "Had we not better take
both boats?"

But there was no time for that, for just as we
had unlocked the padlock and jumped into one
of them, someone, hatless and shirtless, came
tearing round the bend of the rocks. It was
the brutal Bill, and in an instant I noted that he
was unarmed. He was evidently a man of
prompt action, for without uttering a word he

rushed headlong upon me like a wild animal, as I stood on the edge of the natural quay. Pete was a little to one side taking aboard the heavy chain that secured the boats. On came Bill with the glare of a savage creature in his eyes. So great was the light from the burning hut that I could see his features distinctly. I waited until he was within a couple of feet of me, then, springing quickly aside, put out my foot, tripped him up, and in another second he had pitched, with a great crash, head-first into the boat. I thought the fall must have killed him, and swamped the boat, for it plunged down in the bows until the water ran in over the sides. But Pete evidently did not want to be burdened by the carcass of the smuggler, for he promptly jumped into the boat after him, caught him by the feet before he could make a move, and tipped him over the side into deep water.

"Jump in, Wally, for goodness sake!" cried my comrade; "they'll be on us in another second. Crikey! here they come! No time to trouble about the other boat—in with you and row for all you're worth."

I jumped in and, seizing an oar, shoved off; at the same moment three or four smugglers came rushing down towards the quay. As we passed under the archway *ping! ping!* went a couple of revolver shots, and the bullets flattened against the rocks close to our heads. Just as we cleared the archway and shot out into the lake the wild crew of desperadoes had reached the quay. *Ping! ping!* went their revolvers **again**. *Whiz-zip!* went the bullets. But either **that** lurid wild light was deceptive, or they were **too** excited and full of rage to take the careful **aim** necessary to make good shooting with a revolver, for although one or two of the shots struck **the** boat they did no harm to us. I noticed that **the** second boat in the meantime had drifted from the quay towards the archway. Pete and I now crouched in the bottom of our boat, and taking an oar I used it as a scull. We noticed that some of the smugglers were helping the hapless Bill out of the water by means of a boat-hook. The smuggler-chief himself stood for a moment on the quay, the very picture of impotent rage. His legs were apart and he shook his clenched fist at us like a maniac.

"Oh, you fools!" he shrieked; "O, you devils! I'll make you pay for this! I'll roast your bodies over a slow fire until there's nothing left of you but your bones! You'll not escape us!"

In another moment he had dived from the quay and made for the drifting boat. He succeeded in catching it up, clambered in over the side, made back to the quay, and was joined by three of his fellows. They shipped the oars and immediately their boat shot through the archway in hot pursuit.

"Git up, Wally, and row like mad!" cried Pete. "It's some years since I took a turn at the oars in the old Mississippi, but I reckon I can make a fair show yet. We'll give them jokers a heat for it anyhow, and die game if we hev' to."

We bent to our work and the boat churned through the water. It was quite evident that the smugglers meant to take us alive—why, it was not difficult to guess, seeing that Campbell had pretty clearly defined the situation. The still-house was now one great white column of flame, which shot high into the air, lighting up the horrible gulch as with the glare of noon-day, and eclipsing the wan light of the waning moon and stars. The wild birds rose from the neighbouring islands in a panic of fear, and filled the night with their clangorous voices. We could hear the unearthly howls of the coyotes and timber-wolves from the shores.

We had about seventy yards of a start on the smugglers, but unless we could increase our lead the outlook was rather a hopeless one. Besides, there were four of them, so that they could take turn-about at the oars, while there was no rest for us. It was our intention to make as nearly as possible for the cave in which we had first found the boat, jump ashore, and rely upon our fleetness of foot to out-distance the smugglers in the rough, wild pine-clad country. The chances were, however, that should they think we were going to escape them, they would fire a volley into us and the game would be up. It was a case of life and death, so we strained every nerve in our bodies, and shot along at a spanking pace. In another minute or two we would be out of the still water and have rounded the last of the outlying islands. "Pull, sonny, pull!" cried poor Pete, as he bent to his oar like a man possessed. "Never say die!"

But I saw to my dismay that the smugglers were gaining upon us. In a few minutes more we would be in their power. And now Campbell, the smuggler-chief, stood up in the bow of his boat and watched us intently. He was excited to an extraordinary degree and behaved just like a maniac. He shook his fist at us and laughed in a way that made our flesh creep.

"Stay with it, boys!" he cried to his men, " we're gaining on them, and soon we'll have their bodies roasting on the embers of their own fire,"—he raised his voice as he cried out to us— "Ho, there! you silly fools, you may as well save your wind and knuckle under—you haven't got the ghost of a show!"

To this invitation Pete and I made no reply, but rowed all the harder with the energy of despair. We shot past the point of the last of the islands and stood out for the open waters of the lake. Suddenly that weird dazzling light, which had so startled me several minutes before when on the island, burst out again somewhere ahead of us, but it was no momentary flash this time.

Instinctively Pete and I turned to look at it. What we saw was a sight that neither of us are likely to forget to our dying day. There, within two hundred yards of us, were a couple of large rafts, each with a species of lug-sail bellying to the breeze, and slowly drifting down upon us. Upon them stood a large number of men. It was evidently a magnesium light that was being burnt so as to give the occupants some idea of their proper position. My heart throbbed wildly as in the fierce white light I could make out distinctly the kharkee uniforms, slouch hats, and long boots of Mounted Police troopers; and the leather trappings and picturesque gearing of the cowboys. We could see them looking at us and our pursuers in evident astonishment.

"Hurrah!" shouted Pete, "Pull like mad, Wally! Thank God we're saved!"

But the smugglers did not intend to let us escape so easily.

CHAPTER XX.

THE GREAT FIGHT.

WHEN the smugglers realised that they were running right into the lion's mouth they backed-water instantly, and stared at their much-dreaded enemies, the police, with amazement and consternation. But only for an instant, for with a cry like a wild beast that has been balked of its prey, Campbell raised his revolver, levelled it at us, and fired. Fortunately Pete and I had divined his intention in time and ducked, so that the two bullets he sent on their way went whizzing over our heads. The smugglers put about and made back the way they had come. In another minute we were alongside the raft, and the next thing I knew was that Colin Dunbar, the rancher, was wringing my two hands in his as if he meant to do me bodily harm. The good man seemed so overcome at our unexpected meeting that he was quite unable to speak. In another moment the police officer whom I had met at Waller's appeared. With self-possession and readiness that with him had become second nature, he leapt into the boat, calling on three of his men to follow him.

"You come, too, Dunbar," he cried; "and as for you," indicating Pete and myself, "give up your oars to those who are fresh, but stay in the boat. We'll want you to pilot us to the lair of the real spirits of these parts. We must take these chaps alive if we can. Sergeant-major Wilde, try and place the two rafts one on each side of the island, land the men, keep them well under cover, and await further orders. Lay to, boys!"

In less time than it takes to write it, two brawny troopers were pulling together with a long measured stroke that sent the boat flying through the water. Everything had happened in such an inconceivably short space of time, that it seemed almost like the incongruous turn of some vivid and fantastic dream to be chasing our late pursuers. It was turning the tables upon them with a vengeance. The magnesium light that had burned on the raft had now gone out, but the glare from the burning hut still shed a weird lurid light on the deep mysterious waters, and threw the rugged pine-crested islands into bold relief. The smugglers made back for their stronghold even more quickly than they had set out from it. We could see the gaunt figure of the smuggler chief as he sat in the bow of the boat, his hands gripping the sides, his head slightly bent forward, watching us with a peculiar concentrated stare. He reminded me of some huge ape, behind the bars of a cage, which, having spent its strength in a wild

paroxysm of rage, was lying back in a state of impotent senility.   He did not attempt to fire at us,
but once or twice he seemed to rouse himself, and
shook his fist at us in a way that would have
been ludicrous had it not savoured of tragedy.

As our boat churned through the water, Pete
and I told our story to Colin Dunbar and the
officer of police in as few words as possible, and
described the physical peculiarities of the smugglers' retreat.   It transpired that one of the notes
put by me in the bottle and consigned to the
lake, had been found some days previously on a
strip of sand by the western cliff.   It had been
discovered none too soon, for in another twelve
hours the search party would have left under the
belief that Pete and I were both dead, and our
bodies lying in some inaccessible spot in the
Land of the Lost Spirits.   They had lost no
time in withdrawing from the observation of the
smugglers so as to throw them off the scent, and
in building rafts in a secluded cove.

Our boat was fast catching up on that of the
smugglers, but in another hundred yards the
latter would gain the archway and then they
would to a large extent be the masters of the
situation.   The two troopers bent to their oars
right bravely, but it was of no avail.   The smugglers, with something that sounded like a wild
howl of triumph, passed under the archway, and
just ere they did so, the smuggler chief seemed
to recover something of his old vindictiveness,
for levelling his revolver at us he fired, and one

of the troopers dropped his oar with a bullet through the fleshy part of his right arm. Immediately his place was taken by another man.

"Hold hard," cried the officer of police, there's no use exposing ourselves more than is necessary to those wretches, who know well enough it means the gallows for most of them even if they don't get shot. We'll surround the island when the rafts come up and take them all in good time. In the meantime we'll take care that no one tries to escape. Nicholls,"—this to the trooper with the injured arm—" you'll be rowed to the raft as soon as it comes up and Dr. Haultain will see to your wound. It was fortunate we brought the doctor with us. I wouldn't wonder, by the way, if these scoundrels could account for the mysterious disappearance of Dunthorne about a year ago."

We stood out from the shore and waited for the rafts to come up. By the light of the still blazing still-house we could see the smugglers running up from the little harbour towards the remaining huts. It was quite evident they were barricading themselves in, and making preparations for a siege. They might as well shoot a few policemen and cowboys, seeing that in any case their lives would be as good as forfeited. The rancher had ripped open the trooper's coat sleeve and was binding it up until such time as the doctor appeared upon the scene. In order that one of the rafts should be stranded at the far end of the island near the kitchen-garden, we pulled slowly round in that direction ; we would thus be able to signal it on its arrival. We were passing the high rock where our late prison was, when looking up towards the great gap which Pete and I had so lately made in the stone wall, and from which our improvised rope of blankets still dangled, we saw in the imperfect light the dim figure of a man making frantic signals to us. Who on earth could it be, and what were the designs of this person ?

" Don't go too near," I counselled, the past threats and cunning of the arch smuggler-chief occurring to my mind at that moment, and visions suggesting themselves of a keg of gun-power with a fuse attached being dropped into our boat should we approach too near.

But to our surprise we saw the man, apparently unarmed, swarm down the rope until he dangled from it with his feet just touching the water.

" Here's something queer," exclaimed the officer. " Pull in, but be very cautious. He's a dead man if there's any treachery."

A few strokes from the oars and we were close to the swaying figure.

" Alan ! " I exclaimed in astonishment, for it was indeed the smuggler who had all along been our friend, and doubtless to whom we owed our lives, when on the first day of our arrival the ballot-box was called into requisition.

The police officer caught him by the nape of the neck and pulled him into the boat.

" Dunthorne ! " he exclaimed, with a look of

incredulity and amazement which also found a reflection on the faces of the others. " In the name of all that's wonderful, how did you get here ?"

" I came here much as these two did," he replied. " I was taken prisoner, and to save my own life agreed to join them. I had to swear never to betray them, and I have kept my word. But I made a stipulation that they were never to expect me to pull a trigger or lift a hand against the uniform, and in return I promised never to lift a hand against them. Should my name not already be struck off the strength of the force, you will surely not ask me to go back upon my word. I have been watched like a prisoner myself all those weary months. What would the force have gained if I had been shot ? Can you tell me my position now, sir ?"

"You are Corporal Dunthorne still," replied the officer, " and we'll put you on board the raft. You have been the victim of circumstances, and the Commissioner is a just man. You have my sincere sympathy, and I am sure you will have his."

The officer shook him heartily by the hand, and the action was immediately followed by the others. It was with no little emotion that Pete and I did so also. This man's personality, which had before been such a mystery to us, was now made plain enough. In a few words I told the officer of police how undoubtedly he had saved our lives more than once, and how he had befriended us all along.

In a few minutes more one of the large rafts

15

came bearing down upon the island. The great lug-sail bellied to the breeze, and loomed up vaguely, like some uncanny thing, in the lurid half-light. As it was let down it flapped and shook with a noise like muffled thunder. The raft ran into the little bay by the kitchen-garden and grounded on the beach. We signalled it and pulled alongside. Immediately the men sprang ashore. The trooper who was shot through the arm was handed over to the police surgeon, who had with him all the necessary surgical appliances, and our friend Alan Dunthorne, smuggler and non-commissioned officer of police, was left to assist him. Pete and I were given revolvers apiece, with a belt of ammunition, and were told by the officer to keep in his neighbourhood and that of the rancher, but on no account to expose ourselves to the fire of the smugglers, as naturally they would blame us for all their troubles.

By this time the second raft had pulled in to the rocks on the east side of the island, nearly opposite the little glade and pathway that led down from the burning still-house. The men spread out until a species of semi-circle was formed opposite the hut in which the desperadoes had entrenched themselves, but not within a hundred yards of it at the nearest point, as there was the clearing to reckon with; not to keep well in cover of trees and rocks meant certain death.

The officer, who was a plucky fellow, crawled

forward under the scanty cover of the rickety shed and called upon the smugglers to sur- render. But the only reply was a couple of bullets fired into the rotten shanty that caused him to beat a discreet and prompt retreat. Then an order was given by the officer to fire a volley upon the hut, but the damage done was evidently slight. Then from their log strong- hold several little jets of flame spurted out in irregular succession. A cowboy who had, after the manner of cowboys, somewhat recklessly exposed himself from behind a tree, dropped like a stone with a bullet through his leg. He was borne away at considerable risk by another cowboy and a trooper.

"The deuce take them!" muttered the officer, who was now close to me under cover of a large pine. "I'm afraid they are going to give us some trouble. They must have done something worse than make whisky in their time or they wouldn't stand out like this. What sort of hcaps did you say they were like, Derringham?"

"The sort of brutes who take a delight in thrashing boys, sir," I replied. "They laid me on the ground and flogged me with a rope the very first day I was here, because I cheeked them."

Then I blushed for myself in the dark, because surely now I was something more than a mere boy. At least I thought I was.

The officer laughed. "Served you right for cheeking your elders—Goodness!"

It was my turn to laugh now. A bullet had

made the bark fly close to his head; he ducked in rather an undignified fashion.

"Those chaps are no tender-foots," he remarked, thoughtfully.

It was a picturesque if tragic scene—the blazing hut, the little stronghold from which jets of flame kept darting; the clear piece of encircling ground, on which to venture meant death; the dusky group of encircling pines where the sharp ring of the unseen troopers' rifles spurted out the death fire; beyond that the gleaming lake with its dark isles; above that those great, gloomy, encircling cliffs, and above all the luminous grey-green of the heavens, in which the stars were beginning to go out one by one, just as the lights disappear in a great city at peep of day.

It was beginning to get piercingly cold, for a sharp frost had set in, and in a day or two we knew that there would be ice on the Lake of the Lost Spirits.

"I say, Derringham, this won't do, you know," remarked the officer, "you're shivering with cold, and there's hardly room behind this tree for both of us. Creep to the bank and find Dunbar, or your late friend in misfortune—the man with the business eye, and the nose that looks two ways at one time—"

"Broncho Pete is as good-looking as you, sir, or anyone else when you get to know him!" I interrupted hotly.

"Keep your coat on, Derringham," laughed

the officer. " I quite agree with you. It's only the little way we have of talking out here, and merely meant to save any demonstration of affection."

I thought of Pete's quaint " Wally, old stock--ing," and knew that there was something in what he said. I stammered out an apology and crawled back to the bank. I was not long in finding the rancher, who seemed to have been anxious as to my safety.

" We'll wait the end here together, Derringham," he said, " it can't be long now—something's pretty sure to happen. Their ammunition is bound to run out, but just before that they'll make a break, you'll see."

We soon found out how true his words were. Suddenly, as if he had just recollected something, he said again—

" By the way, I had nearly forgotten. You won't guess what I've got here for you, Derringham ? "

I looked at his face and I did guess.

" It's a letter from the Old Country ! " I cried.

" Yes," he replied, and after fumbling in an inside pocket for a most absurd time, he pulled it out. " I thought it was just possible you might like to see it when we found you."

I almost snatched it from his hand. I knew that, excepting my uncle Gilbert, there was only one other person who was likely to write to me, and that was my girl friend, Muriel Wray.

" Is it from her ? " asked the rancher smilingly.

and watching my face. I had mentioned her existence to my friend.

"Yes, sir," I answered, and somehow could not help blushing, simply because it was from a girl and not from a boy. Then I felt ashamed of myself for being so disloyal, and strove to make amends.

"But she's one of the best sort of girls I ever met, sir, a regular brick, and quite as good as most fellows!"

"Don't apologise for her," remarked Colin Dunbar dryly, "I'm quite sure from the little you've told me that she doesn't require it. Put that letter away, there's something going to happen now, and no mistake. Just look there!"

He sprang into an almost upright position. I thrust that dear letter into my pocket and looked too. It was a remarkable sight that met our gaze. Some adventurous trooper had set fire to the coarse, dry grass in the open. A great gushet of fire ran quickly down to the lee side of the log hut. In a minute more a pile of firewood and rubbish close to the gable end had caught fire, and in two minutes more the whole place was aflame. A triumphant murmur of voices from the troopers and cowboys was heard.

"Stand to your posts, men, and look out," cried the officer.

"They are going to make a rush for it," cried Colin Dunbar. "Now, stick to me or the Inspector, Derringham, and don't be rash. By Jove, they're coming out!"

CHAPTER XXI.

TO THE DEATH.

WHEN the stronghold of the desperadoes burst into flames, their fusilade stopped abruptly, and immediately the officer passed the signal to his troopers and the cowboys to cease firing also. Why they should have wasted ammunition in firing upon that strongly-built log-hut at all was a mystery to me. The only vulnerable part of it was the roof, which was composed of birch bark, and was now ablaze. Surely the time had come for the desperadoes to surrender. The troopers closed in cautiously to the edge of the clearing, the grass of which was burning like a miniature prairie fire. Indeed it was difficult at times to see the hut at all through the lurid murkiness. It was a wild, picturesque scene, but one which I would not care to see again. It was a terrible thing to think of those misguided men rushing on so recklessly to their grim fate. Suddenly I heard a voice at my elbow—

"I say, Wally, old stocking, don't you be a gittin' too near. Them coves are only foxin'. They're up to some devil's work, you kin bet your boots."

And Pete was right, for in another second, with a blind, wild helter-skelter rush the desperadoes made a break for one of the rafts. It was doubtless their idea to push off from the shore, hoist the lug sail and let it drift with the wind. It was a mad idea at the best, for before such a slow and clumsy contrivance as a raft could get clear of the shore, it was tolerably certain that the fugitives would be shot down.

Bang, ping! bang, ping! and as they ran the smugglers faced about and fired upon such of the cowboys and troopers as came too close upon them. But the desperadoes had somewhat the best of the start, for what with the burning grass, the smoke, the uncertain lurid light, and the fact that they had made their exit by a back way, a good many of the troopers and police hardly realised at first that the enemy had fled. But they very soon found out, for as I ran with the officer through the burning grass and blinding smoke towards the huts, we could hear the ominous rifle and revolver shots ring out, and the hoarse voices of the men as they rallied to the pursuit.

How that flame scorched my face and hands, and how that black smoke suffocated us as we stumbled blindly through it! Pete and Colin Dunbar had attempted to follow, but a gust of wind just then swept up an impassable barrier of flame in their faces, and they were obliged to desist. When the fire caught the drier and ranker grass among the trees, and the whole island was ablaze, it was every man for himself, and that meant a rush for the rafts. Then no one knew where his comrade was, and confusion for the time being reigned. It was a nightmarish, fitting scene for the Land of the Lost Spirits.

The officer and I quickly passed the burning huts, and as we passed over the slightly rising ground beyond, we saw three of the smugglers keeping the police at bay, while a couple of them endeavoured to push off the raft upon which was the surgeon and the wounded trooper. The sight startled me.

"There are only five of them there," I cried. "Campbell, one of the others and Make-Thunder have escaped somehow!"

A sudden thought struck me.

"They've made for the little harbour where the boats are," I cried. "If we take this boat down here and row round, we could stop them."

It was only too true. When the huts were practically surrounded, no one thought of the smugglers' boat in the harbour. So while one lot of the smugglers ran one way, Campbell, Bill and the Indian, with the cunning of foxes, ran another, and they did not run in vain, for there was not a soul to prevent them from jumping into the boat and pushing off.

The officer and I rushed down to the remaining boat, which luckily, the desperadoes had not seen in time, and jumped in. Another trooper followed us, and without waiting for further assistance we pushed off. The trooper and I took an oar apiece, making the boat fairly spin through the water. We rounded the rocks, and there, some two hundred yards ahead of us, was the only other available boat, with two white men and an Indian in it, steadily making its way between two islands in the direction of the canyon.

I really pitied the officer when he saw how completely he and his men had been outwitted, just when it seemed that he had as good as effected a capture.

"I'll never forgive myself," he groaned. "It is the greatest mistake I ever committed in my life! And to think that we had them as good as surrounded! But we must capture them, I can't go back without them. They can't go farther than the head of that canyon, anyhow, no matter how long it may be."

He sprang from his seat in the stern.

"Give me that oar, Derringham," he cried. "You've done enough for one night, anyhow."

I gave it up to him, and to tell the truth, I was not sorry. The strain of the past twenty-four hours had almost been too much for me.

It was a wonderful dawn, that in the Lake of the Lost Spirits; as we sped through the water I had an opportunity of observing it. The wan light streamed in like one vast shaft over the high, dark eastern cliff, and the great gulch of black waters was filled with that luminous grey-ness that one only sees during a thunder-storm.

Looking back I could see a red glare showing through the dark, straggling pines on the two little islands we had just passed. It looked like an angry dawn in a world of gloom, but I knew it was only the flare of the burning buildings and the grass in the fastness of the outlaws. I realised then to the full the truth of the scriptural saying—*The way of transgressors is hard.* I thought of one of the men—Campbell—we were then in pursuit of, and of his misspent life, and it occurred to me that probably it was the seeds of insanity that had allowed him to drift so easily into his evil courses. I told the Inspector of his mad fancies, but he said nothing. Goodness knows I owed the smuggler-chief no debt of gratitude, but is it not better to err on the side of mercy—if erring it be?

On, on we sped, over the dark waters and through the chill morning air.

"Are we gaining on them, do you think, Derringham?" cried the officer, with something that sounded almost like a ring of entreaty in his voice.

"I think so, sir, in fact, I'm pretty certain of it. You see, the Indian can't row, and the other two have to do all the work, and they are pretty well played out."

It was as I said. Already I could distinguish the occupants of the boat more clearly, and I knew that it was not altogether owing to the increased light. And now the great cliffs began to draw in upon us on either side, until at last we were in a species of canyon. How high those cliffs were! Looking upwards and then down at the water, was to make one feel giddy. And how deep was the black water beneath us. There was no strip of shore on either hand—not a broken piece of rock on which even a cat could gain a foothold. To come to grief there meant saying good-bye to this world.

On, on we sped. Was the canyon going to pierce into the bowels of the earth for ever? The cliffs were now so high, and came so close together, that it seemed as if twilight had again settled down on the face of the waters. Suddenly I thought the distance between the two boats had considerably lessened.

"Let me take your oar, sir," I begged, "they are getting played out. You'll be able to keep an eye upon them better. It is Campbell, Bill, and Make-Thunder, and you'll have to be very careful."

I daresay it was presumptuous on my part to tender such advice, but I knew the men from experience.

He allowed me to take his place; he then took his position in the stern with a rifle in his hands. It is one of the regulations in the police force, that firing on a criminal must only be resorted to as a very last resource. The canyon now became so narrow and tortuous that at times we lost sight of the desperadoes altogether, but still we were gaining upon them. Suddenly with a warning shout the officer cried—

"Back water! back water, for goodness sake! We're right on to them!"

The trooper and I obeyed with all the strength that was left in our bodies, but that did not prevent us running full tilt into the fugitive's boat with a force that sent me sprawling backwards. When I picked myself up I was alone. The other boat was empty, and lay close against the foot of a rough ledge or incline, exactly like a bridle track, that ran upwards into what seemed the other world of light and day. But great boulders had fallen from the cliff above right on to it, distracting the eye and thus preventing me at first noticing the human figures, some hundred feet or so above, who were about to take part in the last scene of a stormy drama. And then the sharp ring of a pistol-shot made me look more closely until I could see plainly what was going forward.

When the desperadoes had reached the ledge, they had jumped quickly ashore, leaving their boat to its fate, and it was when suddenly rounding the bend that ours had crashed into it. They ran quickly up the steep and shelving slope, but the police by this time were close at their heels, and they knew that there was nothing for it but to surrender or fight.

Campbell faced about and fired one shot out of his revolver at the police inspector, but his aim was wild, and the bullet went wide of its mark. The police being determined to take their quarry alive did not shoot. Then the desperate smug-

Q

gler-chief called upon the brutal Bill and the Indian to stand and fight. From motives of prudence Bill stood his ground and kept the police at bay with his revolver. But the Indian, with a series of long strides, kept on. Infuriated by this exhibition of cowardice and disobedience, Campbell, with almost superhuman agility, bounded after him and caught him in his arms. It was only at this juncture that I properly saw what was going on owing to a turn in the ledge. The sight was such a strange and terrible one that, while it lasted, Bill, the pursued, and the police merely stood still and watched. It was one of the shortest and grimmest wrestling matches I ever saw in my life.

Make-Thunder, my old would-be assassin, wriggled round quickly when he found himself in the smuggler's grip, and flung his arms over and about the latter's back, after the most approved manner of wrestlers. Then, for at least two minutes, the two spun round furiously on the brink of that terrible abyss. Now the smuggler would draw the Indian to him, and lift him off his feet. Then the Indian would manage to free himself, and the spinning would begin again. But at last the end came. Campbell had managed to force Make-Thunder close to the edge of the precipice, when suddenly freeing himself from his grip, he struck the Indian a terrific blow on the chest that sent him spinning over the brink. It was then the police made a rush in upon Campbell. But the smuggler-chief had as little intention of being taken prisoner as of going over the cliff in the embrace of a red-skin, for turning towards his would-be captors with a mocking grin on his face, he made them a low bow, and sprang into that nightmarish abyss. It was a sickening sight to see his body pass through the air. I tried to shut my eyes, but I could not; the sight seemed to fascinate me. So perished this strange man, and with him, probably, the secret of his downfall.

But the end of the drama was not yet. When the police rushed in upon Campbell, Bill, seizing his opportunity, made a dash past them, and came thundering down the slope. He knew that if he could only kill me, push off with the two boats, and round the corner, he was saved, and his two opponents outwitted with a vengeance. My revolver lay in the stern of the boat, but I had no time to pick it up. The police, some seventy or eighty yards behind him, dared not fire lest they should accidentally shoot me. I seized an oar, determined to receive my old friend Bill in the only way that I thought would impress him. He had evidently made up his mind to make very sure of me, for he did not seem in any hurry to fire. But he delayed too long; just ere he reached the water's edge he stumbled and lurched forward. Now was my opportunity. Before he could recover himself I stood up in the boat, swung the oar over my head, brought it down heavily on his thick skull, and in another instant he fell all of a heap, senseless into the boat.

"Well done, Derringham! Well done, my boy!" cried the officer, as he and the trooper reached the boats. "You've made a capture, anyhow, and retrieved our fortunes. If you haven't broken his thick skull he'll make a brave show in hand-cuffs and leg-irons!"

They placed him in an easy position in the boat in which he had come: the trooper taking off his coat and placing it under his head; and then, knowing the desperate character of the man with whom they had to deal, they took the precaution of making fast his feet and hands.

I confess that though this was the man who had treated me so brutally, I almost felt sorry for him, fearful lest my blow had killed him. It is not a pleasant thing to think that you have killed any one, even in self-defence.

"Can't you do anything for him, sir," I asked. "Put some water on his face—try to bring him round, or something of that sort?"

The officer shook his head.

"It's no use," he replied, "you'll see he'll come round soon enough. Get him back to where Dr. Haultain, our surgeon, is, that's the best thing, I think. Roberts," turning to the trooper, "you stop in the boat with him, and Derringham and I will tow you back to camp. It's well on in the forenoon now, and they'll be wondering what's become of us. It will be four or five o'clock before we get back. Derringham, let me shake hands with you."

I could not exactly see what there was to shake hands about, but I shook hands with him all the same.

During that long row back, despite the stormy events of the past twenty-four hours, I kept wondering what was in Muriel Wray's letter. Though I was dying to read it, the very thought that it was safe in my breast pocket was wonderfully comforting.

About four in the afternoon, dead tired, we reached the island. What had happened in our absence?

CHAPTER XXII.

AFTER THE STORM.

WHEN we drew near the island our comrades saw us coming, and hurried down to the little harbour to see how it fared with us. The first to greet me was Colin Dunbar, who seemed vastly relieved when he found that I had suffered no mishap. No less solicitous was my old friend, Broncho Pete—old, I say, for a friendship in captivity, even if only for a few weeks duration, must be more calculated to draw kindred spirits together than years of ordinary intercourse. Pete's manner of showing his pleasure at my return was characteristic of the man. He seemed to have an horror of being demonstrative.

"Hello! Wally, old stocking," he exclaimed, looking at me critically, with his business eye, " bin havin' a good time?"

"A lively one, anyhow, Pete," I replied, "all that I know is that I'm precious hungry. Where's the commissariat department?"

"Pierre's kitchen and store be still to the fore, thank goodness!" he replied, "otherwise it would have gone pretty hard with us, you bet."

The first thing the officer and I did was to have a good wash, and go up to the kitchen, for it was about twenty-four hours since we had broken our fasts. Four of the troopers were sent with the two boats to the mainland, where the police camp was, with orders, and to get some necessaries. I was happy in the thought that Bill, whose head I thought must have been broken by my oar, had returned to consciousness, and like most brutal men and braggarts, was now reduced to a condition of mind bordering on cowardice. When I caught his eye, however, as he was assisted out of the boat by two troopers, he looked at me as if sorry he had not flogged me to death that time when I was at his mercy in the still-room.

It was a lucky thing, indeed, that Pierre's kitchen and store had escaped the flames, otherwise it would have gone hard with the victors for food, seeing that the two rowing boats had been so unexpectedly called again into active service. While we sat in Pierre's kitchen having something to eat, the sergeant-major, to save time, came in and made his report to the inspector. We were then joined by Colin Dunbar, and were soon in possession of all that had occurred during our absence.

When the smugglers endeavoured to seize the raft, it was as much as the police could do to frustrate their designs. The smugglers had at first made a bold resistance, a regular hand-to-hand fight taking place. At last, however, they were overpowered, but not before several casualties had taken place. Two policemen and one cowboy had been badly wounded, while a couple of the desperadoes had been shot dead, and the others more or less injured. They had only managed to save Pierre's kitchen and store with the greatest difficulty. A regimental cook was at once put in charge of it. The still-house was an almost unrecognisable heap of smouldering ashes, while the hut where the smugglers had made their last stand was also burned to the ground.

The two dead desperadoes, by descriptions in the possession of the police, were identified as notorious outlaws from the States. Over the heads of each had hung warrants for apprehension on charges of murder. I was glad to hear that our late jailor, Jim, and Pierre had only been slightly wounded. As nothing of a criminal nature was known against these two, save their smuggling transactions, and their resisting the police under arms, it was more than likely that they would get off with a limited term of imprisonment in Stony Mountain Penitentiary, Manitoba. They had taken their capture in such good part that the police had not thought fit to put leg-irons or hand-cuffs on them as they had at first intended.

I told the officer that it was their votes in the ballot-box that had doubtless been instrumental in saving Pete and myself from being shot, and I also testified to the kindly treatment received from both. It was only right that some distinction should be made between them and the others. I had the satisfaction of learning that their considerate attitude towards us would not be forgotten, but be in their favour when on trial.

As for Jim, the sergeant-major related a rather characteristic incident regarding him. He had shown himself a model prisoner until ordered by his guard to remove some of the grime and smoke from his face by going down to the lake and having a good wash. But to this Jim objected, by saying that it was only three days since he had washed, and he did not quite see the necessity of washing again since the chances were he would be just as dirty again in twenty-four hours. Being ordered down to the lake, he dipped a corner of the towel in the water, and applied it so gingerly to the tip of one ear that his jailers could stand it no longer. He was seized by a couple of brawny troopers and a bucket of water poured over his head.

As for Bill, he was recognised as an old offender against the law, and kept heavily ironed until lodged in a Mounted Police guard-room.

And all this time Muriel Wray's letter was in my possession and unopened. I was simply dying to know what it contained, but still such had been the stirring sequence of events that it was impossible to snatch five minutes for its perusal. Besides, I wanted to be quite alone when reading it—in some place where I would be free from all distractions. As soon as we had finished our much needed meal I made my way quickly towards my old prison-house, the cave. I noted that the police and cowboys had made their respective camps on the eastern side of the island on an unburnt patch of ground. How black and grimy everything looked! What a change had come about in the smugglers' stronghold within the past twenty-four hours!

It was with mixed feelings that I entered that cave of my own free will from which only some seventeen hours before I had risked my life in order to escape. There was something so incongruous and unique in the situation that it savoured of unreality. There was the rope of blankets still dangling over the ledge, and there was the tin dish out of which I had last eaten. When the police and cowboys had made their attack on the island on the previous night, Alan had stolen the key of the great door and taken refuge there, so as to be out of the way according to his agreement with the smugglers.

Seating myself on an old tarpaulin I took out the letter and read. There was nothing very wonderful about her handwriting, compared with that of most boys it was very ordinary writing indeed, the most that could be said for it was that it had a certain daintiness and was free from blots.

It began by saying how glad she was to

receive the letter I had written her on my arrival at the ranche, and how fortunate Mr. Dunbar and myself must have been to escape the ambush of the Indians as we did. Of course, she had told my uncle everything about my running away, not forgetting her own share in the matter. At first he was undoubtedly distressed, although he did not say much before the other members of his family. He had gone back to his books, but could evidently get no comfort even from them. He had come to her and said that if I would not come back I might at least be all the better for some money, and he handed to her a substantial sum saying that there was no need for anyone to know anything about it. But the girl had declined the money saying that she did not think I stood in any immediate need of it. There could be no doubt, she wrote, that my uncle Gilbert was very fond of me, although it was not in his nature to show it. There were other members of the family, she hinted—and I believe she was having a sly dig at me—who were not far behind him in that respect.

She went on to say that I could not be sufficiently thankful to have fallen in with such a good friend as the rancher, Mr. Dunbar. He must be a very dear man indeed, and she had quite taken a fancy to him, merely through what I had said in my letter. I could if I liked give him her love (I vowed I would do nothing of the sort—compliments or kind regards, perhaps, but not her *love*). Of course, she had missed me, and the Cedars did not seem the same since I had gone. Was I aware of having left a little silver pencil upon the shelf in the old summer-house, where she had found it? Well, she had taken possession of that pencil, and would keep it safely until some day I returned. The handing it over to me would be something to look forward to.

Then she went on to give me all the news relating to the Cedars, and such things as interested me most. I could not have believed it possible that any girl could have entered so fully into what practically constituted my life. It was indeed a revelation; but when I thought of those great uncanny eyes of hers, my wonder ceased. I had sometimes seen a look in them as if they had solved the mystery of life and death. It was a bright, cheery letter, the sort of letter in which there was not a line that did not make me feel that the writing of it was a labour of love.

And then came the most extraordinary news of all—a piece of news that fairly took away my breath, and seemed to change my entire worldly outlook. Why she kept it back to the very last, as if it were merely of minor importance, it would be difficult to say, unless the mysterious and seemingly contradictory workings of a woman's mind can account for it.

Did I remember the apparently worthless shares that my father had left me in a gold mine at Charles Tower in Queensland? They had been doing nothing but spending money on that mine for years, sinking a shaft to try some reef. Well, they had struck it at last and a great reef it was, three feet thick and full of gold. The shares that before were hardly worth holding had gone up to fabulous prices in the market, and my uncle calculated that I was now worth twenty thousand pounds at the very least. He was writing to me himself, and my aunt had graciously said that now I could come home if I liked, and they would try and make things comfortable for me.

I smiled on reading of this change of attitude in my aunt, as, doubtless, the girl must have smiled when she put it down on paper.

But if she, Muriel Wray, might be allowed to express an opinion, she would not advise me to come back just yet. What could I do if I were back? It would be the greatest mistake in the world to settle down to a hum-drum, idle life in England before I had had any real experience of the world. If I liked the life I was now following, why not stay with my friend Colin Dunbar for a few years, so that I might at least aspire to the dignity of one who had worked for his living? What title to the dignity of manhood could a drone have who had done nothing all his life save loaf about a club in town or shoot partridges in the country? She herself was going to travel about on the continent for a year or two with an aunt. She would always write to me, and she hoped I would always write to her.

In two years she would come back to England, and it would be jolly if I could manage to take a trip home then and we could meet again. And then she wound up by expressing the hope that I would take care of myself, and not forget there were those who had an interest in my well-being.

I laid the letter down, and it was some time before I could realise its import. A few days ago a penniless boy—to-day one with independent means! Had I not much for which to be thankful. But without experience of life and knowledge of the world there were dangers of money as my girl-friend had pointed out. If I could not realise to the full the truth of this myself, I knew that what she said must be right —she had always been right, and her motives were disinterested. Truly her friendship was something more precious than gold! Her advice would be followed to the letter, and meeting her again would be something to look forward to.

I had hardly noticed that it was getting dark, so leaving the cave I found my friend Colin Dunbar in a tent which had been brought from the police camp on the main-land. I at once told him of the news contained in my letter. It somewhat surprised me to find he did not betray any particular elation over my good fortune. There was a thoughtful look on his face. I asked him if he did not think it was a piece of good luck.

"It may and it may not be, Derringham," he

answered. "I've got a theory that no one should have money until he's worked for it and knows its value. It is largely by comparison that we appreciate things. Perhaps, there is no man more to be pitied than the one who is born with a silver spoon in his mouth; he seldom knows of what metal that spoon is made. And besides, I suppose you'll want to clear out now and leave me. Well, I suppose it's only natural. It would have been better for you, I think, if that money had just come a little later."

"It's very good of you to speak like that," I said; "but I haven't the slightest intention of going back just yet. Indeed, I'm only too glad to be with you, and I like the life."

Then I told him what my girl-friend had said in the letter, and while I took the opportunity of expressing my gratitude to him for his goodness to me in the past—he cut me short when I touched on that point—I said that if he could see his way to let me buy a small interest in the ranche he would still further increase my sense of obligation to him.

This seemed to please him immensely. He clapped me on the back and seemed greatly relieved.

"I always thought you had some sense in your noddle, Derringham," he exclaimed, "and now I'm sure of it. Ever since that morning when you tackled the thief at the coffee-stall in Covent Garden, I thought you were made of the right stuff, and I've never been disappointed in you

once since.   Money or no money I'd have taken
care that one of these days you didn't want for
an interest in the ranche.   As for buying a
share, there need be no hurry about that.
When you form a better idea as to the value of
ranching property, and your uncle can get some
one whom he can trust to advise you, we'll see
to it.   In the meantime I'd keep the news to
yourself.   By the way, you and Pete are pretty
sure to get a reward from Government for being
the means of leading the police on to the
smugglers."

"Then Pete and Alan can have my share,
sir," I said.

And when some months afterwards the
grant was allowed, despite their protestations,
they had it.

One other man I had to tell of my good
fortune was my old friend in captivity, Pete.
Since knowing him I had conceived the greatest
respect for his many sterling qualities, his
invariable cheerfulness, and even some of his
little eccentricities.   Finding him in the cowboys' camp I took him aside, acquainting him
with my good news.   He was eating a piece of
bread and meat with his clasp-knife when I
found him; as I spoke he went on eating.   Then
deliberately finishing the bread and meat, he
delivered himself thus—

"Wally, old stocking, I wishes you luck; but
remember though money's a mighty good thing
to have if you use it properly, it's a mighty bad

thing if you don't. I think you'll use it properly, sonny."

It was arranged that next day after a thorough examination of the island we should all leave it, and make our way back to the open prairie country, where we would say good-bye to our friends the police. That night I shared the rancher's tent, and surreptitiously slipped my friend Muriel Wray's letter under the saddle-bag that served me for a pillow. Just ere I fell into a sound sleep, a girl appeared at the open tent door and look at me with a smile upon her face. It was a beautiful face; and was framed in a wealth of gleaming hair which hung down loosely over her shoulders in great silky waves; it was of the colour that the setting sun leaves behind it in the fleecy clouds after the rain. But it was her eyes that fascinated me; they were dark and limpid as are the deep pools in a brook. And as they looked into mine they became instinct with kindliness. Smilingly she lifted one hand as if in greeting. I stretched out mine to her. But the vision faded away as fades the gauze-like morning mist before the rays of the rising sun, and in another minute she was gone.

R

CHAPTER XXIII.

SIOUX INDIANS ON THE WAR-PATH.

ON awakening next morning, before the full dawn of consciousness, I experienced in my heart the old sense of heaviness borne of captivity. But the roof above my head was of canvas and not of stone, and the voice I heard was that of Colin Dunbar bidding me good-morning instead of my jailers ordering me to get up. And then the glorious truth came home to me that I was once more free, and no longer the prisoner of a godless, desperate set of men who any moment might take my life. It was indeed a blessed relief to think of it.

The police and cowboys were early astir, for much had to be done that day. A thorough examination of the island had to be made; the police inspector had to prepare notes for his report, and all had to proceed to the main-land, and if possible make the prairie country before sunset.

It was indeed a lovely morning, and already the sun was peeping over the high eastern cliff. There was not a cloud in the sky—there seldom is in the North West Territories—and the air was crisp and bracing. The wounded men were progressing favourably, and the light-hearted troopers and cowboys were joking and laughing as if there was no such things as danger and tradegy in the world. I sought out Pete and bade him good-morning, for strangely enough I experienced a sense of something wanting when his cheery greeting did not fall upon my ear with a note of comfort in it on awakening. It was not altogether on account of my freedom and unexpected good fortune that made me feel so light-hearted and in such a charitable frame of mind on this particular morning. It is more than likely that Muriel Wray's letter, and the fact that I was now in a position to pay her back the twenty pounds borrowed from her, that had something to do with it.

Going over to where the prisoners Jim and Pierre were with their guard, I wished them both good-morning. Jim vouchsafed me a surly nod, but the little French-Canadian seemed as usual in the best of spirits and greeted me as he had always done with smiles and bows. I told them that I would beg permission of the officer to allow them to smoke, whereupon even Jim expressed his thanks if in a somewhat shame-faced fashion. I could see, however, that there was something on his mind which with his usual awkward reserve he hesitated to put into words. Asking what it was he wanted to say, he replied—

"It's that there washin' business, sonny; if you could just manage to ask the boss to let me hev' my way in thet, I could be doin' without the baccy. Hevin' to sluice myself in thet cold water twice a day—ugh!"

"Get out your towels," interrupted a grinning trooper at this point, "and we'll go down to the lake where you'll make yourselves beautiful."

A look of supreme disgust came over Jim's face on hearing this speech, but he shouldered his towel all the same, and with the smiling Pierre walked down to the lake-side followed by his armed guard.

For an hour after breakfast the police officer was busy with his inspection of the island, and drew out a full report regarding what had occurred. While he was thus engaged the two boats had been employed taking the troopers and the cowboys with their belongings to the mainland. Colin Dunbar and I stopped until the inspector had completed his work. It was with mingled feelings I went to my old prison-house, the cave, and glanced around me for the last time. It is wonderful how the human mind can adapt itself to circumstances, and it is more wonderful still how it can look back with something almost approaching to a sneaking regard even upon a prison cell. Doubtless, some subtle phase of the law of association may account for this. Truly I had learnt some valuable lessons in that cheerless spot, and I recognised their value.

It was with a light heart I left the island next day, in the last boat with the inspector, Waller and Colin Dunbar.   It was difficult to think that only a few weeks before Pete and I had approached it, as curious as two children, with our stolen boat.   So much had happened since then that I seemed at least a couple of years older.

The boats were hauled up high and dry by the troopers and covered with a huge tarpaulin.   It was more than likely they would again be wanted in the spring.   Then began our rough march over the rock and pine-covered plateau to the subterranean ravine that led down from the Land of the Lost Spirits into the free and boundless prairie country.   At last we stood on the long ridge, like the ruins of a mighty wall, that stretched right on to where we would strike our point of egress.   It was close upon sunset when we stood on the termination of the ridge directly above the ravine, and saw stretching out before us, like a huge coloured map, the open dun-coloured prairie.   There was nothing there to shut out God's sunlight or break the course of the wandering winds as they strayed over countless leagues of rustling grasses and nodding prairie flowers—nothing save the narrow fringe of cotton-wood trees and wolf-willow that marked the presence of some erratic creek, the haunt of the musk-rat and the beaver.   How my heart went out to that great grassy wilderness where the horizon line blended with the blue, and there were no cruel cliffs hemming one in, significant of captivity!

We dropped through the large hole at the bottom of the ravine, and wended our way by candle-light down through the long galleries and tortuous passages, until at last we stood at the foot of the crag on the bare hill-side. In another quarter of an hour we stood on the site of our old camp on the creek bottom. Here we found a couple of drays, and the cook's waggon awaiting us. As, however, the police horses occupied the little valley, Colin Dunbar and Waller resolved to move a couple of miles or so further down the creek and camp on the open prairie, where the two mobs of horses could be kept well apart, and there would be sufficient grass for each. To my great delight I found my old stock-horse Barney in the mob. My saddle and bridle were also intact in the waggon. The rancher told me he had felt so sure all along that I would turn up again, that he had my belongings kept so that I could find them the same on my return. The only injudicious thing he had done was to write to my uncle in the Old Country, acquainting him of my disappearance. He had, however, considered it his duty to do so. When we got to the ranche that could be remedied by sending a letter on to Maple Creek by special messenger.

We moved on in a body down the creek after saying good-bye to our friends the police, and pitched our camp for the night. We were up the next morning at daybreak; the wounded cow-boys were put in the waggons and we began our homeward journey. What a glorious thing it was to be again in the saddle; to feel a good horse pulsating with life underneath one, and to experience that sense of exhilaration and buoy-ancy which only the boundless expanse and ozone-charged air of the prairie seems to give! The rancher and I rode on ahead. There was no trail, only the springy prairie grass under our horses' feet with here and there a bunch of sage-bush. At last the prairie began to get more broken and to roll away in a series of heights and hollows, or, as the cowboys would have expressed it, in buttes and coullees. The sky was clear as any vaunted Italian one, and the day being cool we made good progress. Indeed so fresh were our horses that before long the fact dawned upon us that we must have left the waggons and the cowboys far behind. The rancher had fortunately told them to camp punctually at noon under any circumstances, and lest, as we had anticipated, we found our-selves to be too far in advance of the main body we had taken the precaution of putting some cold meat and bread in our wallets.

It must have been about eleven o'clock in the forenoon, and we had been jogging along side by side for some time in silence, when suddenly I caught sight of something on the opposite side of a little valley that made me draw up quickly and utter an exclamation.

"What's the matter, Derringham?" asked the rancher, who apparently had been deep in some day-dream.

"Look over there," I exclaimed, "on the other side of the coullee—Indians!"

The rancher also pulled up, and shading his eyes with one hand looked long and anxiously.

On the brow of the valley were two picturesque figures on horse-back : Indians in the full glory of war-paint and feathers. The air was so clear that we could see them quite distinctly. Great plumes of eagles' feathers stood up crest-like over their long braided locks ; white ermine tails dangle from the breasts and sleeves of their crimson flannel shirts, heavily ornamented with blue, yellow and red beadwork. Their loose leggings were fringed and beautified in a like fashion. Both Indians, who sat as still as statues, had long rifles slung across their shoulders.

"Sioux Indians on the war-path!" exclaimed the rancher. "What on earth are they doing over on this side the lines ? Up to some mischief, I'll be bound. Let's ride towards them, but keep a wary eye in your head and your Colt's revolver handy on your belt."

The rancher waved his hand as if in greeting to the Indians, and headed his horse down the valley. But they evidently had no intention of being interviewed, for turning round they galloped off eastward. When we reached the brow of the hill they were almost out of sight.

The rancher seemed not a little perplexed and troubled.

"I can't quite make it out," he observed. "I never saw Sioux Indians come over here yet but what there was trouble. Either it was to stir up the Cree and Assiniboine Indians to disaffection, or it was to massacre the whites, or get some scalps from the Blood, Piegan, or Sarcee Indians. I can't think that those chaps we saw are alone. It's more than likely they are merely scouts sent out from some main body; we'd better go cautiously."

How true his words were we were not long in finding out. We kept our spirited horses well in hand and moved along more slowly, keeping a good look-out the while. We had just reached the top of a little ridge when all at once a sight that filled us with wonder and apprehension met our eyes. It was a great body of mounted Sioux Indians on the war-path. They were coming towards us in one long straggling line; one, two, and three deep. The braves came first, resplendent in all their gorgeous and barbaric panoply of war. About half a mile behind came their camp followers driving their *traveaux,* which consisted of a couple of poles slung across the back of a pony, the ends trailing on the ground, with cross-pieces on which rested their camping paraphernalia. A large number of half-wild dogs slunk after the cavalcade.

It was a picturesque sight, the savage red men of the prairie amid his natural surroundings.

When we caught sight of them the foremost of the Indians was not more than a quarter of a mile distant. So struck and surprised were Colin Dunbar and myself by such a large body of warriors that for a good couple of minutes we stood stock still in speechless wonder and admiration. For the moment we hardly paid any attention to the fact that at sight of us a number of braves broke away from the main · body, urging their horses in our direction. The first thing that brought us to our senses, and a knowledge of our impending danger, was the *ping* of a rifle and a bullet that whistled over our heads. In another moment the scene was almost indescribable.

Brandishing their rifles over their heads, and whooping and yelling for all the world like a pack of hounds in full cry, a score and more of Indians came on at full gallop; their small wiry ponies covering the ground in truly marvellous fashion. *Ping! ping! ping!* and as they sat in the saddle they levelled their rifles at us and fired. Fortunately their bullets went wide.

"By jove, Derringham," exclaimed the rancher, "I reckon we'd better get back to dinner at the camp! These chaps don't seem hospitably inclined. Right wheel about, and back the way we came. Our good bronchos can lay their cayuses long odds, anyhow."

We turned our horses, and giving them their heads started off at a rattling pace.

"There's no particular need to hurry, Derringham," observed the rancher. "All we've got to do is just keep a certain distance in front, and we can easily do that; there's no necessity to play our horses out. We'll be at the camp in less than an hour from now. The only thing which troubles me is that there are rather too many Indians for our lot; there must be at least a couple of hundred fighting men amongst them."

This was exactly what was troubling me, for our camp did not number more than twenty men all told, and if the Siouxs were bent on mischief it was extremely unlikely that the cowboys could withstand such overwhelming odds.

Shoulder to shoulder galloped our horses, with long easy strides. They seemed as fresh as when they had set out in the morning. Down valleys and up hill-sides they tore as if possessed, and glorying in the doing of it. How their feet clattered over the stony water-courses, and how they leapt clear of the treacherous wash-outs as if in sheer wantonness! And ever we could hear the hound-like yelp and whoops of the red men as they followed behind us, urging their ponies on to the pursuit with heels and quirt.* Every now and again some enterprising spirit amongst them would send a bullet whizzing over our heads, an earnest of what we might expect on getting within range.

"Stay with it, Derringham," cried Colin Dunbar to me cheerily, we've got them well in hand. It doesn't hurt us and it amuses them,

* Short whip.

so what's the odds!   We'll be at the camp in no time, and that will give those jokers a bit of a surprise.   They're not going to lift our scalps just yet awhile."

I think Colin Dunbar, when in what some men would call a fix, was one of the coolest hands I ever met.   Turning in my saddle at the brow of a hill I looked back expecting to see that some of our pursuers had dropped out of the running.   But to my no little surprise and consternation I found that so far from such being the case, their numbers had been considerably augmented.   There were at least fifty Indians in pursuit, and they were now closer upon us than I had imagined.   Away in the distance, across the valley some few miles off, I could see the main body " lopeing " or cantering up.

"I think we'd better put 'on a spurt, sir," I ventured.   " If you look back I think you'll see they mean business."

He looked and gave expression to his feelings in a low whistle.

"This is slightly more than I bargained for, Derringham," he remarked.   " By jove, I don't know that if when the main body comes up they won't be too many for our boys !   This is getting serious.   Let's get a rustle on."

It was, as he had said, more than he had bargained for. He had, with his men, gone through fighting enough within the last few days to satisfy the most sanguinary minded of

men. Two cowboys at that very moment lay
badly wounded in his waggons, and now a bloody
battle with one of the most warlike tribes of
Indians on the North American continent was
imminent. It never rained but it poured! At
any other time with sides less out of proportion
he would rather have enjoyed the excitement
than otherwise. As for myself, I confess, I did
not care about that bloodthirsty pack at my
heels. Still, I had faith in my horse, Barney,
under me, knowing full well that as yet I had
not pushed him, and he was comparatively
fresh. He was always considered one of the
" stayers " on the ranche.

And now we urged our steeds with voice and
boot, and away they flew over the brown prairie.
It was neck against leather, truly, for should a
horse stumble, or a cinch-strap give, it would be
all up with us, and our scalps would dangle at
the girdle of a Sioux warrior.

" Stay with it, Barney, and make sure of your
footing, old boy¡ "

Ping ! ping ! ping ! and the astonished
Siouxs, when they found that we had been
merely playing with them in the matter of
racing, and that they were being left behind, set
up a series of wild howls, and blazed away at us
with their rusty rifles.

" If only the Mounted Police hadn't left us,"
exclaimed Colin Dunbar as we ran neck for neck
" we'd give them such a dressing-down as they
never got in their lives. That's what they want

badly, and unless they get it now, they'll do it again."

And then, when we rounded a little ridge, and when we least expected it, we rode right on to our camp where the cowboys were having dinner.

"We're all right now," I cried, reining in my horse.

"I'm not so sure of that," remarked Colin Dunbar, grimly; "they're five to one!"

"I wonder if the Mounted Police are still at their old camp," I said.

CHAPTER XXIV.

A RIDE FOR LIFE.

As Colin Dunbar and I galloped into the camp the cowboys, seeing at once that something was wrong, sprang to their feet and grasped their rifles. Their horses were quietly grazing on a good patch of grass on the other side of the creek; being hidden by a thick belt of cotton-wood trees they fortunately escaped the keen eyes of the Indians.

"Now then, boys," cried Colin Dunbar as he drew rein, "here's the Siouxs down upon us. Draw up these drays and that wagon so as to form three sides of a square. Take out the tail-boards and anything at all that will serve to make an inch of cover, and let those fellows see that one white man is worth a dozen Indians any day."

In a moment all was hurry and bustle. The two wounded men were lifted out of the drays and placed in the middle of the square. Four men ran some couple of hundred yards to the belt of cotton-wood trees, and returned with a couple of large logs which they laid on the ground. The tail-boards were fixed in position by means of an axe and some tent-pegs, and every preparation for a laager was speedily made. Colin Dunbar had jumped off his horse and was himself assisting.

An idea had suggested itself to me, and its origin was in the question I had asked the rancher, as to whether he thought the police had yet moved their camp or not. Colin Dunbar had said he feared the Indians might prove too many for the cowboys, which, of course, meant that he considered a bloody massacre not improbable. If the police had not shifted camp they were not more than ten miles away at that moment. There were between twenty and thirty of them, and if they could only come to the rescue, they would give the Siouxs such a lesson as they never had before. For even the sight of a red-coated, mounted policeman is more than enough for most Indians. Being all men of superior physique, splendid riders, good shots, and mostly dare-devils, the red man has found to his cost, more than once, that they are not to be played with. What was to prevent me going back to our old camp in search of them, and bringing them to the assistance of the cowboys? The latter could at least hold out for some hours, and in less than two I would be back again.

It would be a risky thing to do, truly, for if the police had shifted camp and I could not pick up their trail quickly, the chances were that the Indians, some of whom were pretty sure to follow me up, would eventually run me down.

But it was better to risk my life in a cause that
commended itself to all that was best in me
than to remain inactive and perhaps witness the
total extinction of our party. I knew that if she,
my girl-friend, were asked to decide upon my
course of action, she would unhesitatingly have
told me to think of others first, even if it carried
with it my death sentence. My mind was made
up; I would delay no longer. Going over to
where Pete was, I briefly communicated to him
my intentions, and turned my horse's head so as
to be off before they could stop me. As I rode
away I could hear Pete stammer out—

"I say, look here, Wally, old stocking,—"

The rancher cried—

"Derringham, where in all the earth are you
going to?"

"To the police camp for help," I shouted back.
"Barney's fresh, and I'll be there in no time.
Stand them off till I come back."

Just at that moment I heard a wild series of
whoops, and, looking over my shoulder, saw a
large body of Indians come sweeping round a
wave-like piece of rising ground at full gallop.
They did not make straight for the laager of the
cowboys, but, as is the custom in Indian warfare,
they spread out in single file in order to close in
upon their intended victims, by describing a
series of ever-narrowing circles round the camp.
Their horsemanship was admirable. Some of
them seemed to lie flat on their barebacked
steeds, while others, twining their long legs

s

round the necks of their ponies, leant back on the near side, and fired shot after shot at the enemy, so that from the camp the riders could hardly be detected. And all this while they were riding at full gallop. Then I heard the ring of Colin Dunbar's Winchester, and I had the satisfaction of seeing a horse with its Indian rider fall headlong on the prairie. It was quite evident, that for some considerable time at least, the cowboys could very well take care of themselves. But I had heard of the courage and dogged pertinacity of the Sioux warriors, and I knew that not until the greater number of them had bitten the dust were they likely to cease the attack.

"Now then, Barney," I cried, "give them a lead," and in another moment I was off in real earnest.

"*Tally-ho!*" It was a glorious race, and my blood warmed to the work. I could hear the yells of the Indians as they saw me set out on my lonely ride, and I knew that two or three of the braves had left the main body so as to follow me up. "Let them all come!" The more of them the better; it would relieve the attack upon the camp, and it would be a most impressive piece of melodrama to ride into the Mounted Police camp with a score or so of Sioux Indians at my heels. The police would be surprised, but the Siouxs would be still more so. They would wish they had stayed at home in their wigwams to abuse the squaws.

"Stay with it, Barney! Show these wild bronchos of the plains what a difference a drop of good blood makes in the spirit and in the staying power!"

Barney shook his head, tossed his mane, and settled down to his work as if he thoroughly understood what was required of him. *Tally-ho!* A spin with a good pack of hounds across country is all very well, but a ride for life on a half-bred broncho across the trackless prairie with a pack of yelling Sioux Indians at one's heels is excitement enough to satisfy the most jaded palate. *Tally-ho! Yoicks!* It is an odd experience to find oneself in the place of the fox; straining every nerve and muscle so as to get clear away, and wondering if there will be a chance of trying conclusions with the first hunter who is in at the death.

On, and still on, over the rustling prairie grass and glaucous-hued sage-bush; over the bare, white alkali flats, and over the flint-strewn watercourses. What a devil's tattoo the hoofs beat on the dry bed of the creek! and what an unearthly yelling goes up from the human pack of hounds as poor Barney stumbles over a partially concealed badger-hole and comes down on his knees, sending me spinning over his head! Surely my scalp is already as good as hanging at the belt of the Sioux brave who is in the lead!

I pick myself up, quicker than ever I picked myself up in my life, rush to my horse, and catch it by the bridle rein. But the Sioux warrior is right on top of me. I can see the flecks of foam upon his reeking steed, and the pulsating of its red nostrils. There is a blood-thirsty glitter in the Sioux's brown, almond-shaped eyes, and his rifle is brought to his shoulder. Have I to suffer death at the hands of a red-skin after all? Not if I can help it!

Before he can pull the trigger my large-sized Colt's is drawn from its pouch and levelled full at his head. Next moment he throws up his arms and comes down all of a heap over his horse's neck.

Bang, bang! and two bullets whiz past, perilously close to my head. Throwing myself on Barney's back, I dig my heels into his sides, and off he goes again like the wind. There is a mad clatter of hoofs behind me, as with voice and lash the Indians made a great effort to run me down. If they catch me now it is not the friendly bullet that will do the final work, but the stake and the lingering tortures of fire and knife.

"Stay with it, Barney. Give them a heat for it, my boy!"

And shaking his head and mane again, my plucky steed strikes out with new life. But there is an Indian close at my heels who will not be shaken off. He is some young brave, who, having only just passed through the ordeal of the sun-dance, is anxious to distinguish himself by lifting his first scalp. It is a meritorious ambition no doubt, but that scalp shall not be mine! Unless I stop him, he may stop me by sending a bullet through my back at any moment. It is no time for sentiment.

I draw my revolver again, turn in my saddle, and not a moment too soon, for he is close upon me. But the gaudily bedecked youth seems such a youth—no older, I fancy, than myself— that even in the heat of pursuit it is not in my heart to risk killing him. Lowering the muzzle of my revolver, I pull the trigger, and his horse lurches forward wildly with a bullet through its brain, and the young brave measures his length upon the prairie. He will have to defer taking scalps until a more convenient season. But I feel glad that I did not kill him.

And now I pass the camp of the previous night, two miles more and I shall know my fate. What if the police have left? But I had heard the police officer say that he thought a day's rest after the rough journey over the plateau would do the wounded men good; I can only hope that he continued to think so.

One mile more, and I enter the little valley. If the police are not in it, then I am caught like a rat in a trap, and my scalp may dangle after all at the girdle of the Sioux. I hear the jubilant voices of the hounds behind me as they laugh to themselves over the simple manner in which I have run myself to earth. My heart sinks within me as I look up and down the little valley. There is neither sign of man

18

nor horse in that lonely spot! The Mounted Police must have shifted camp after all! Oh, the bitterness of that moment?

But I push on, round the belt of cotton-wood trees, and there, in a group with horses saddled and carbines slung across horn of saddle, and all ready to draw out of camp, are my good friends the North-West Mounted Police. With a wild shout of joy I gallop up to them. In another minute three red-skins come tearing round the bend.

"The Sioux Indians," I cried; "they have attacked the camp, and if you don't hurry up it will be too late!"

"Prepare to mount!" cried the officer.

In another moment every man was in the saddle with his rifle in his hand. And then with an ironic cheer the police advanced to welcome the sorely astonished Indians.

I do not think that ever in my life I saw a foe so taken aback. They had ridden right into the lion's mouth with a vengeance. The police spread out on either side of them, and, literally, before one could say "Jack Robinson," they were surrounded. But Sioux Indians are not so easily taken prisoners. They pulled up their reeking ponies and gazed about them in astonishment, then, realising what had happened, caught up their rifles. But the moment they did so three Winchesters rang out, and the Indians were flung over their horse's heads.

It was a great pity to have to shoot their

horses, but, perhaps, it was better than shooting the Indians. Two of them, when they had risen to their feet, allowed their rifles to lie on the ground, and threw up their hands in token of submission. But the third Indian, who had stuck to his rifle, was in the act of putting it to his shoulder to aim at a trooper, when *ping !* and he dropped it again with a bullet through his arm. In almost less time than it takes to write it, the two Indians were handcuffed together and left in charge of the teamsters.

"Better take that spare horse, Derringham," cried the officer, "and come with us. It is just possible we might take the wrong branch of the creek or something of that sort. I daresay you're tired, but you've got to make an effort."

I was indeed tired, but I flung my saddle on the horse the teamster had picketed hard by, and handed him my plucky little Barney. The officer waited until I had mounted, and then we cantered after the troopers.

Then it was back again the way I had come only a few minutes before. Truly, it was a strange turn in Fortune's wheel; but of late so many startling events had followed so closely on one another that I had almost ceased to wonder at anything, and took whatever came as a matter of course.

The officer and I took the lead, and away we went at a swinging gallop. Our horses were fresh, and as the mounts of the North-West Mounted Police are the best to be had in

Canada, we covered the ground in splendid fashion. But would we be in time to succour the cowboys from their perilous position? Twenty cowboys were all very well, but when it came to a hundred and fifty Sioux Indians and more, the odds were against the cowboys. Still, knowing that I had gone for help, it was not unlikely that Colin Dunbar and Waller would simply act on the defensive, and not allow their men to expose themselves more than they could help. Having plenty of ammunition and being good marksmen, it was more than likely that they had succeeded in sending many good Indians to the happy hunting-grounds beyond the blood-red sunsets.

We passed the spot where I had shot the pony under the young brave, but that gentleman himself was not to be seen. He was doubtless travelling down the creek to join his comrades, in cover of the undergrowth, inventing some plausible lie to account for the disappearance of his steed. Then we passed the riderless horse of the Sioux Indian I had shot. It was grazing peacefully within a few hundred yards of the spot where lay the body of its master. The sight saddened me, and I confess the congratulations of the police inspector jarred on my ears painfully. But it had been the Sioux's own doing; I had only acted in self-defence, and the lives of others depended on my safety.

At this place I pointed out to the officer that it would be as well to cross the creek, and ride down it on the other side in cover of the timber, as otherwise the Indians would see us coming and make off. It was necessary to teach them a drastic lesson if we wanted to live in that part of the country with any degree of safety. We crossed over and rode on in silence. Soon we could hear the sharp ring of rifles and the whoops of the Indians. It was with a sense of relief that we became aware of the fact that the fight still continued. Had there been silence we might have feared the worst. We passed the little herd of horses belonging to the cowboys, and were glad to think they had not been driven off by the Siouxs. When nearly opposite the spot where the unequal fight was going on, we re-crossed the creek, and forcing our way through the timber, halted a moment to take our bearings and prepare for the surprise of the enemy.

It was a striking and significant sight that met our gaze. Riding in a great circle round the entrenched position of the cowboys was a large body of Indians. As we afterwards learned, they had tried more than once to rush in upon the position of our friends, but each time had been met by a fire so deadly and so withering, that they had been forced to retire and take up a position some few hundred yards distant in cover of some rising ground, where they could rest and prepare for another attack. With the exception of one or two slight casualties the cowboys had held their own, but their ammunition was becoming exhausted. Unless help came within the next half-hour or so, their last cartridge would be expended, and their lives forfeited to the pertinacity of the Sioux warrior. It was quite evident that, maddened by the loss of several of their comrades, the Indians meant to force their position by sheer strength of numbers. And now they had begun the attack again, and were closing in with an ever-lessening circle upon the waggons. It was high time for the police to act.

"Now then, men, to the rescue of our friends," cried the officer; "and let those red-skins see that they cannot play at this sort of game with Britishers with impunity. First gave them a volley at two hundred yards, standing. Pick your men if you can, and take care of the waggons. At the word of command you will mount, and give it them hot. Now then, *dismount. Fire !*" And five-and-twenty rifles belched forth the death-fire.

"Now then, prepare to mount—*Mount !*"

And with a ringing cheer the police dashed forward.

CHAPTER XXV.

"ALL'S WELL THAT ENDS WELL."

WHEN the police fired a volley, standing, at the circling Siouxs, several of them reeled in the saddle and fell headlong from their horses. Still, it was such an unaccountable surprise that for the moment the main body of horsemen continued their wild career. They could hardly realise what had happened. When, however, the police charged upon the Indians in *échelon*, meeting the whirling horde as it came round man by man, they realised. They were taken at a disadvantage, for to meet a foe face to face was hardly in their programme. They could not stop their onward course to take careful aim, and so those who pluckily raised their rifles to fire upon the police made but poor shooting. One police horse was all they managed to shoot. On the other hand, the troopers, when they came abreast of their enemies, suddenly pulled up, and each picked off his man as coolly as if practising at the butts. At the same moment the cowboys—who had up till now been lying flat on the ground behind their cover, firing a volley into the Indians whenever they attempted to carry the position by storm—rose in a body and poured their last round into the wavering Indians.

That settled the matter: one or two of them, with the well-known intrepidity of the Sioux, made a bold dash at the new-comers, and strove by voice and action to rally their comrades; but it was a foolhardy and futile endeavour. They had not advanced many yards before they fell headlong to earth, and their riderless steeds went careering over the prairie. They drew together in a little body and prepared to resist the police—for even now they outnumbered their adversaries by three to one; but, before they could do any harm, their antagonists with a wild cheer charged in amongst them and scattered them right and left. It was the old story of the disciplined few against the undisciplined many.

One trooper in the meantime had run up the horses of the cowboys; a supply of ammunition was speedily served out to them, and mounting their horses bare-backed, the cowboys joined their allies, the police. The Sioux warriors were so much amazed at this sudden rallying of their intended victims, that the inevitable demoralisation set in, and soon they were in full flight. But their ponies were now tired, while the mounts of their pursuers were comparatively fresh. Never were braves on the war-path so thoroughly discomfited and routed as they were.

Away they went helter-skelter with the police and the cowboys at their heels. Away, over the rolling prairie; down into deep creek bottoms—where the forces of nature must have been going on for countless ages to make such scars on the surface of an old ocean-bed—and again up steep hill-sides, where startled coveys of prairie chickens that had been strutting about in the sunshine flew away with a whirr at their approach. Away, amongst wave-like heights and hollows, where timid bands of antelope stood at gaze for a minute or two, with that remarkable spirit of curiosity which those shy creatures evince, before bounding off again with the fleetness that no horse can equal.

Such of the Indians as resisted arrest were promptly disabled or killed. In most cases they had their horses shot under them, and a few men coming up behind made them give up their arms, which were at once smashed to pieces over rocks and stones to save further trouble. The owners were herded together as prisoners. It was a sad down-come for the high-spirited cavalcade that Colin Dunbar and I had seen that morning riding over the prairie in the bright sunshine, in the full glory of war-paint and feathers.

The pursuit continued till well on in the afternoon; only one or two thoroughly exhausted and badly scared Indians succeeded in escaping. They rode back foodless by weary stages to their own country, in the neighbourhood of Pine Ridge, to warn their fellows against again venturing into the country of the red-coats.

The other Indian prisoners were next day taken under escort of Mounted Policemen into the fort, from which place a wire was sent to the American authorities by way of the Rocky Mountain Telegraph Company's line to Fort Assiniboine.   From there a troop of cavalry was sent to take the Indians back to their own country, for John Bull and Uncle Sam on either side of the lines, have always worked most cordially and harmoniously together in order to preserve peace and order in the vast territory under their respective charges.

It was long after sun-down when the last policeman returned to camp with a tired horse, the significant trophy of a beautifully wrought and beaded head-dress, and a pouch for holding "kinakinink"—a species of dried willow bark which the Indians use as tobacco.   The re-union between the police and the cowboys was most cordial and one for congratulations. Owing to the prompt and effective measures which Colin Dunbar and his men had taken to protect themselves from the fire of the Indians they had in no way suffered, unless one or two slight casualties from spent bullets and ricochets could be taken into account.   But the police had not arrived a minute too soon, and when I thought of the part I had played in helping to prevent what would have doubtless been a terrible catastrophe to my friends, I experienced a sense of satisfaction such as I had rarely before known.

If I had wandered away in a spirit of idle curiosity into the Land of the Lost Spirits, and occasioned them much inconvenience in searching for me, I had at least helped to break up a gang of desperadoes, whose illegal doings had for long been a curse to the country. Moreover, and I say it in all humility and with the full consciousness of my youth and inexperience, I had been largely instrumental in bringing about a sharp reprisal on a dangerous body of Indians, whose bloody raids had long been a menace to a comparatively unprotected country. Now, it was pretty safe to say, such raids would not be likely to occur again.

Colin Dunbar and Waller were jubilant; such a lesson as had been taught the Indians, who had for years been killing their men and running off their horses and cattle, had long been desired, without any hope of realisation; but now the much-needed lesson was an accomplished fact, and a lengthy period of peace and security were assured. The rancher had taken me on one side when I returned to the camp, for I was too played-out to go in pursuit of the Indians, and, putting one hand upon my shoulder, said—

"Derringham, it's no use saying much, but I think you've more than earned the right to purchase that interest in the station you spoke about. You'll have it as soon as we get back to the ranche, and at a price that no one will be able to call in question. Should the money never be forthcoming it won't matter in the very

least, for I've no one else to give anything
to, and I've much more than I'll ever require."

I thanked him and felt there was at least
someone who considered that, so far, my short
career had not been without some measure of
success. I determined that the satisfaction born
of the knowledge of something accomplished
would not be allowed to die for want of a little
effort in the future.

That night it was very cold, and the stars
gleamed brightly in the blue. We had moved
our camp close to the creek, amongst the cotton-
wood trees, for shelter, and till late in the night
the police and cowboys sat round the great
camp-fires talking and recalling incidents of the
attack and pursuit. I was so dead tired, however,
that I had soon to seek my blankets, and I fell
sound asleep almost as soon as my head touched
the bundle of dried grass, tied up in my towel,
which served me for a pillow. I did not dream
of being pursued by yelling Indians, but of a
beautiful old house in a quiet English county
where life went smoothly on from day to day,
sweetly and peacefully as a summer's dream,
but where the people did not realise it, because
they had never known anything else. I had not
realised it once upon a time, but I did now.
Truly, as Colin Dunbar had said, the enjoy-
ment of things is largely a comparative quality.

That night a picket-guard of five men kept
watch over the prisoners. Next morning several
of the cowboys accompanied the police to assist

them in conveying the prisoners into the Fort. Colin Dunbar, Waller and I pushed on to the ranche, which we made on the following day. There was nothing to fear now, for the only lot of dangerous Indians who were likely to do any harm had been broken up. How comfortable and homelike did the roomy dwelling-house at the ranche seem after the rough state of affairs I had of late experienced. There were my slender belongings just as they had been left, only it seemed years since I had seen them instead of only a few weeks.

There was a letter awaiting me from my uncle Gilbert Derringham. It was quite a long one for him to write, and couched in kindly language. He regretted that I had thought it necessary to leave the Cedars as I did, but that was now a thing of the past, and need not be referred to again. He told me of my good fortune in regard to the Queensland mine, and said, as those whose opinion was most valued by me said, that although I was now practically independent, if my heart was in my work, it would be a fatal mistake to give it up to lead an aimless existence. My friend Muriel Wray had hinted that I might like to purchase, if it were possible, an interest in the ranche of my friend Mr. Dunbar. He thought it a good idea. A couple of years' work would give me a better title to the dignity of manhood. At the end of that time it would be advisable for me to pay a visit to the Old Country. In the meantime, as my

T

trustee, he would see to my affairs. My aunt and cousins desired to be remembered to me.

Upon the whole it was a satisfactory letter, although I smiled on reading the message from my aunt and cousins. Well, the world had taught me that it was better at times to forget certain things.

That night Colin Dunbar and I had a long talk as to our future plans. Much as I loved the Old Country I recognised the truth of what my friend said—that at least a couple of years spent in the life I had taken such a fancy to would do me all the good in the world. At the end of that time I could take a trip home, and then circumstances would decide as to my future course of action. Colin Dunbar told me of his project to increase his stock and make the ranche one of the largest affairs of the kind in the province. It would be a good investment for any little money I might put into it. In two years he reckoned the value of property and stock would experience a great increase. Next day, he said, he was writing to my uncle concerning me, and promised to mention the matter. I ventured to express the hope that in the event of Cook, the foreman on the ranche, leaving, he—the rancher—might consider my friend Broncho Pete worthy of the position. Whereupon he said Cook was leaving, and he considered that Pete was indeed the best man for the position. When I afterwards told that rough diamond of my impending connection with the ranche, and, by way of a joke, expressed the hope that I would prove a good "boss" to him, there was a twinkle in his business eye—

"You'll *have* to be, Wally, old stocking," he remarked, "and you bet I'll see to it."

And he was as good as his word, but then Pete was different from anyone else.

Next morning I wrote to my uncle, and then, with a sense of pleasure that, I confess, letter-writing seldom gave me, began a long letter to my girl friend, Muriel Wray. There was, indeed, much to tell her, but I purposely passed over what was likely to make her apprehensive as to my future safety. The rancher had advanced me a draft for her loan of twenty pounds, which I now enclosed. She must take my thanks for that on trust; it was so difficult to express one's sense of gratitude in words. I had read her letter more than once, and felt that what she advised me was the right thing to do; I had, indeed, already taken steps to do it. I told her a good deal about my friend Colin Dunbar, and of his kindness to me. I also told her of Broncho Pete, and of his heroism while in the hands of the smugglers. I was surely privileged to enjoy the company of such men—men whose conceptions of life had been ennobled by its dangers and difficulties. I told her of the rancher's plans, and what we intended doing. I liked the life, but questioned the wisdom of remaining away too long from civilisation. Two years would soon pass, and I would come back to the Old Country again. She had been such a good friend to me all along that I hoped our friendship would continue in the future. If she would write every month I would write to her. It made such a difference in one's life to feel that there was someone who really had an interest in it. It was not because I had no one else to write to, but because I thought we had a good deal in common, and were meant to be friends.

A few months before I would not have admitted as much, but a great deal had happened since then, and I now saw things differently.

I finished my letter, and lifting my eyes from the paper looked out of the window to where, far off, I could see the valley run down into the prairie and wander away towards the dim horizon line. And as I looked a shadowy face rose up before me. Gradually it grew upon the sight and took form and colour. It was a beautiful face that looked out from amid the wealth of falling hair which, flooded by a shaft of sunlight, gleamed like burnished gold. The soft brown eyes looked into mine, and the pure soul of the girl shone through them. They lit up as with a promise of glad expectancy, and there was a smile upon the lips. Then the face wavered and vanished into air. But I knew that in the spirit my friend had been with me.

CPSIA information can be obtained at www.ICGtesting.com
Printed in the USA
LVOW05s1729100614

389432LV00010B/579/P